MATERIALS MANAGEMENT

By

Prof. (Dr.) A.K. SINGH

B.E. (Mech.), M.Tech. (Industrial Engineering) I.I.T., Delhi
PGD(MM), PGD(OM), Ph.D. (Mech. Engg.)
Raj Kumar Goel Engineering College
Pilkhua, Ghaziabad, U.P.

UNIVERSITY SCIENCE PRESS
(An Imprint of Laxmi Publications Pvt. Ltd.)

BANGALORE • CHENNAI • COCHIN • GUWAHATI • HYDERABAD
JALANDHAR • KOLKATA • LUCKNOW • MUMBAI • RANCHI
NEW DELHI

Published by :
UNIVERSITY SCIENCE PRESS
(*An Imprint of Laxmi Publications Pvt. Ltd.*)
113, Golden House, Daryaganj,
New Delhi-110002

Phone : 011-43 53 25 00
Fax : 011-43 53 25 28
www.laxmipublications.com
info@laxmipublications.com

First Edition : 2008
Reprint : 2010

OFFICES

© **Bangalore**	080-26 61 15 61	© **Chennai**	044-24 34 47 26
© **Cochin**	0484-237 70 04, 405 13 03	© **Guwahati**	0361-254 36 69, 251 38 81
© **Hyderabad**	040-24 65 23 33	© **Jalandhar**	0181-222 12 72
© **Kolkata**	033-22 27 43 84	© **Lucknow**	0522-220 95 78
© **Mumbai**	022-24 91 54 15, 24 92 78 69	© **Ranchi**	0651-221 47 64

UMM-9492-090-MATERIALS MANAGEMENT-SIN
C—828/09/11
Typeset at : Kalyani Computer Services, New Delhi.
Printed at : Mehra Offset Press, Delhi.

CONTENTS

PREFACE

This book on "Materials Management" is an endeavour to help the students of Manufacturing Technology Degree course, Mechanical Engineering course and all other engineering degree courses at the level of B.Tech., M.Tech., Ph.D., MBA, BBA, CS, GATE Entrance Examination.

This book has been written in a simple and lucid language so that the students and faculty may understand the concept of the topic clearly. Latest information and techniques have been introduced in various topics. The author has tried to give the information which is essential as per the present scenario.

The author feels highly indebted to Hon. Shri Ajay Singh Chauthala, Member, Rajya Sabha and Chairman, Jan Nayak Ch. Devi Lal Vidyapeeth, Sirsa, Dr. S.S. Dalal, Vice Chairman, Vidyapeeth, Sirsa, Dr. J.P. Singh, Secretary R.C.I., New Delhi, Mr. S.N. Sawroop, Member Secretary Indian Institute of Public Administration, New Delhi, Dr. R.P. Singh, Ex. Dy. Director A.I.C.T.E., New Delhi, Professor (Dr.) Arun Kanda, Prof. (Dr.) S.G. Deshmukh, Mechanical Engineering Department, I.I.T. Delhi, Prof. Prem Vrat, Vice Chancellor U.P.T.U., Prof. P.C. Pandey, H.O.D. (Mech.), I.I.T. Roorkee, U.P. Dr. R.S. Singh, Ex. Chief Agriculture S.F.C.I., New Delhi. Prof (Dr.) R.C. Maheshwari, H.O.D. CRDT I.I.T, D. Hon. Shri Ajay Raj Sharma, Ex. Director General B.S.F., New Delhi with whose inspiration this book has been written.

Any suggestion for the improvement of the book will be welcomed.

AUTHOR

CHAPTER 1

INTRODUCTION

1.1 IMPORTANCE OF MATERIALS MANAGEMENT

1. Materials constitute the biggest single element of cost. Generally more than half the cost of any production system is due to materials alone. Therefore reduced materials cost is vital for improved productivity.
2. Non-availability of materials as resource input leads to production shut down, project delays etc. Hence timely availability of materials is vital for production efficiency.

Materials Management: Some Definitions

1. Materials Management is connected with maintaining adequate supply of something (raw material, spares, components, operating supplies (utilities) to meet anticipated demands economically.
2. The function of Materials Management is to ensure supply of materials at right time, right place, in right quantity, of right quality, from right sources and at right price.
3. Materials Management is concerned with the management of material flow into, through and out of system.
4. Materials Management is confederacy of traditional material activities bounded by a common idea—the idea of an integrated management approach to planning acquisitions, conversion, flow and distribution of production materials from raw material state to finished product state.
5. Materials Management is decision making with respect to design, procurement, storage, issue, packing and handling and accounting of materials to get most out of every amount invested in materials.

1.2 CONCEPT OF PRODUCTIVITY

Productivity is nothing but the reduction in wastage of resources or it is connected with optimal utilization of inputs like men, machine, material, energy, space, time and building etc. for producing goods or services. Productivity of a production system may be defined as ratio between output and input which means the resources utilized.

$$\text{Quantity of Productivity} = \text{Output/Input}$$

Difference between Production and Productivity

Production of any commodity or service is the volume of output irrespective of the quantity and quality of resources employed to achieve the level of output. Once we put an element of efficiency with which resources are used we enter the area of productivity. Thus, production may improve without the corresponding improvement in the productivity and vice-versa. If the input remains the same and the production output increases, there is an improvement in productivity. Production, therefore means the output in terms of money whereas productivity is the efficiency of the system used for production.

1.3 ROLE OF MATERIALS MANAGEMENT

1. Material planning and selection.
2. Purchasing of materials.
3. Inventory storage and stores control.
4. Standardization, simplification and value analysis.

1.4 TECHNIQUES IN IMPROVING PRODUCTIVITY MANAGEMENT

The various techniques to improve the productivity of a system are as under:

1. Task based techniques.
2. Product based techniques.
3. Technology based techniques.
4. Material based techniques.
5. Employees based techniques.

Task Based Techniques

1. Work measurement techniques (time study).
2. Motion study/work simplification(method study).
3. Job analysis.
4. Job evaluation and merit rating.
5. Ergonomics related with human factors.
6. Production scheduling.

Product Based Techniques

1. Product classification and coding.
2. Research and development.
3. Reliability and improvement in product design.
4. Product standardization.
5. Product diversification.
6. Product specialization.

Technology Based Techniques

1. Computer aided design.

2. Computer aided resource planning.
3. Computer aided manufacturing.
4. Computer integrated manufacturing.
5. Computer aided inspection.
6. Group technology.
7. Robotics and just in time.
8. Maintenance management.

Material Based Techniques

1. Material requirement planning.
2. Inventory control.
3. Just in time concept of inventory management.
4. Materials management and quality control.
5. Materials handling systems.

Employee Based Techniques

1. Incentive schemes for individual employees.
2. Incentive schemes for group of employees.
3. Management by objectives.
4. Fringe benefits for employees.
5. Total quality management.
6. Zero defect benefits for employees.

1.5 STANDARDIZATION

Standard is a criterion used for comparison of measurement, quality practiced over a period of time and is established by consent or authority and **specialization** is a brief statement of a set of requirements to be fulfilled by a product, a process or a material indicating appropriate procedure by means of which it may be determined whether the requirements given are fulfilled. So, a specification may be a standard or a part of standard or it may be independent of it.

Standardization means the voluntary fixation of standard dimensions, equipment quality and practice with a view to having a large production of only limited number of varieties or standardization is a process of defining and applying the condition required to ensure that a given range of needs can normally be met with minimum variety in a reproducible and economic way on the basis of current technical know-how.

Purpose of Standardization

1. Standardization helps in establishing the interchangeability of products.
2. With decrease in supervision and allied work the total cost of the product is reduced.
3. It brings uniformity in quality and performance of the product.

Areas of Standardization

1. Within a defined range the physical dimensions and tolerances of components.
2. The rating of infrastructure facilities like machines and equipment may be in terms of units of energy, temperature or current voltage of speed etc.
3. Physical and chemical characteristics or specializations of materials.
4. Methods of testing the properties of equipment keeping in view the minimum precautionary measures and convenience of use.

Advantages of Standardization

1. Standardization reduces the complexity of the manufacturing system.
2. It lowers down the direct cost of manufacture/production.
3. The indirect cost of manufacturing is also reduced.
4. Standardization eases the process of purchase and stock control.
5. The cost of inspection of incoming material is reduced due to standardization.
6. Improved product quality and saving in materials purchase.
7. Workers achieve a high skill and proficiency.

Applications

Specialization is universal in application and it has been applied to *products, processes, machines, jobs, companies.*

Disadvantages. Specialized labour is not flexible, i.e., the switching over from one specialized field to another is not possible.

1.6 COST CONTROL/COST REDUCTION

Productivity can be improved by reducing the production cost. It can be achieved by keeping a close watch over expenditure, by minimization of material wastages, reduction in machine break down periods or idleness of machines, reduction in waiting time for men, power and materials, avoiding excessive material handling and minimization of overtime expenditure.

Value Improvement

For the purpose of cost reduction the usual approach is to manufacture the existing product with less expensive techniques. Value engineering has been proved to be very effective tool of materials management and cost reduction in modern industry. It proceeds with the analysis of the product and then investigates as to how the value can be improved or if the part can be eliminated or replaced by any other part of the same value, i.e., utility or lesser cost. So value analysis looks at the product and investigates into the possibility of performing the same function in a cheaper way. It can be said that the main aim is to study the relationship between the design function and cost of a part, keeping in view to reduce part and its cost through change in design, modification in the specification of the material used by changing the supply sources and so on.

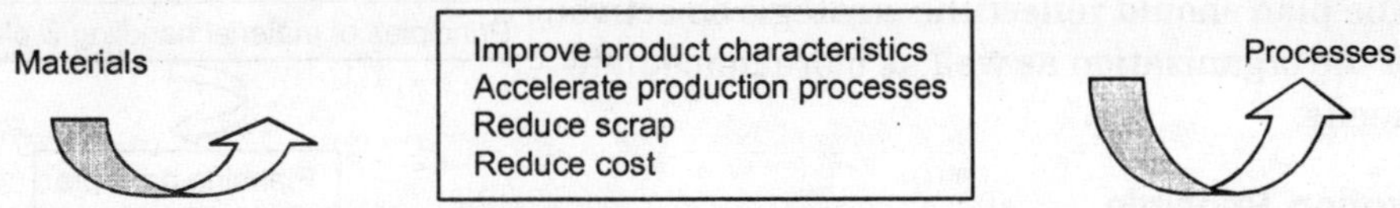

Fig. 1.1 Value improvement

Value Engineering is connected with the efficient selection and utilization of materials. The idea is how to reduce scrap. Reduction in scrap generation may not only affect direct cost of materials which go as waste but it may also reduce the cost of handling, disposal of scrap and storing and saving in space, machine time and labour cost. **Value Analysis** is defined as the process of objectively studying every item purchased or manufactured to eliminate every cost factor which does not contribute to usefulness or utility.

Difference between Cost Control and Cost Reduction

Cost Reduction

1. Existing costs including the predetermined standards challenged in an effort to reduce them. It is thus concerned with genuine cost reduction.
2. The standards are viewed with suspicion. So standards are regarded as measures which can be improved.
3. Changes in costs are expected, therefore the operations of organizations are recognized as dynamic and cost reduction is possible.
4. It is not limited to where standard costing can be applied but can be effective for all types of conditions.

Cost Control

1. Concerned with adhering as closely as possible to predetermined standards.
2. Standards are taken to be the desired state of efficiency.
3. Cost control is guided by conditions, which prevail and lead to lowest production cost.
4. Generally applicable only when some form of standards can be set.

1.7 PRINCIPLES OF MATERIAL HANDLING & PLANT LAYOUT

Planning Principle

1. While making the plan, it should be discussed with the consultant. Planners and the person who is going to get the benefit from the plan is also to be involved.
2. Large scale material handling projects generally requires a team involving suppliers consultants when appropriate and end user specialists from the management, engineering, computer and information systems, finance and operations.
3. The plan should promote concurrent engineering of product, process design, process layout and material handling methods.

4. The plan should reflect the strategic objective of the organization as well as more immediate needs.

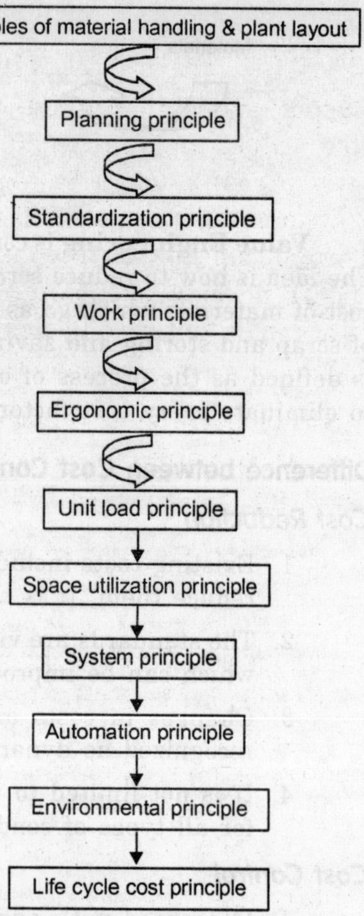

Fig. 1.2

Standardization Principle

1. Material handling methods, equipment controls and software should be standardized within the limit of achieving overall performance objective.
2. Standardization means less variety and customization in the methods and equipment employed.
3. The planner should select the methods and equipment that can perform a variety of tasks under a variety of operating conditions and in anticipation of changing future requirements.
4. The standardization applies to size of containers and other load forming components as well as operating procedures and equipment.

Work Principle

1. Material handling work should be minimized without sacrificing productivity or the level of service required of the operation.
2. The measure of material handling work in flow rate volume, weight or count per unit of time multiplied by distance moved.
3. Simplifying processes by reducing, combining, shortening or eliminating unnecessary moves which reduce work.
4. Where possible, gravity should be used to move materials or to assist in their movement while respecting consideration of safety and the potential for product damage.
5. The work principle is implemented best by appropriate layout planning, by locating the production equipment into a physical arrangement corresponding to the flow of work. This arrangement tends to minimize the distance that must be traveled by the materials being processed.

Ergonomic Principle

Human capabilities and limitations must be recognized and respected in the design of material handling tasks and equipment to ensure safe and effective operations.

1. Ergonomics is the science that seeks to adapt work or working conditions to suit the abilities of the worker.
2. The ergonomic principle embraces both physical and mental tasks.
3. That equipment should be selected which eliminates repetitive labour and which effectively interacts with human operators and users.

Unit Load Principle

Unit loads shall be appropriately sized and configured in a way which achieves the material flow and inventory objectives at each stage in the supply chain.

1. A unit load is one that can be stored or moved as a single entity at one time, such as pallet, container, or tote, regardless of the number of individual items that make up the load.
2. Less effort and work are required to collect and move many individual items as a single load than to move many items at a time.
3. Large unit loads are common both pre and post manufacturing in the form of raw materials and finished goods.
4. Smaller unit loads are consistent with manufacturing strategies that embrace operative objectives such as flexibility, continuous flow and just in time delivery.

Space Utilization Principle

Effective and efficient use must be made of all available space.

1. Space in material handling is three dimensional and therefore is counted as cubic space.
2. In storage areas the objective of maximizing storage density must be balanced against accessibility and selectivity.
3. When transporting loads within a facility, the use of overhead space should be considered as an option. Use of overhead material handling systems saves valuable floor space for productive purposes.

System Principle

Material movement and storage activities should be fully integrated to form a coordinated, operational system that spans receiving, inspection storage, production assembly, packaging, utilizing, order selection, shipping, transportation and the handling of returns.

1. System integration should encompass the entire supply chain. It should include suppliers, manufacturers, distributors, and customers.
2. Inventory level should be minimized at all stages of production and distribution while respecting considerations of process variability and customer service.
3. Information flow and physical material flow should be integrated and treated as concurrent activities.
4. Methods should be provided for easily identifying materials and products, for determining their location and status within facilities and within the supply chain and for controlling their movement.

Automation Principle

Material handling operation should be mechanized and/or automated where feasible to improve operational efficiency, increase responsiveness, improve consistency and predictability, decrease operating costs, and eliminate repetitive or potentially unsafe manual labour.

1. In any project in which automation is being considered, pre-existing processes and methods should be simplified and/or re-engineered before any efforts to install mechanized or automated system.

2. Items that are expected to be handled automatically must have standard shapes and/or features that permit mechanized and/or automated handling.
3. Computerized material handling systems should be considered where appropriate for effective integration of material flow and information management.

Environmental Principle

Environmental impact and energy consumption should be considered as criteria when designing or selecting alternative equipment and material handling system.

1. Environmental consciousness stems from a desire not to waste natural resources and to predict and eliminate the possible negative effect of our daily actions on the environment.
2. Containers, pallets and other products used to form and protect unit loads should be designed for reusability when possible and/or biodegradability after disposal.
3. Material specified as hazardous have special needs with regard to spill protection, combustibility and other risks.

Life Cycle Cost Principle

A thorough economic analysis should account for the entire life cycle of all material handling equipment and resulting systems.

1. Life cycle cost includes all cash flows that occur between the time the first dollar is spent to plan a new material handling method or piece of equipment until that method and/or equipment is totally replaced.
2. Life cycle cost includes capital investment, installation, set up and equipment programming, training system testing and acceptance, operating (labour, utilities etc), maintenance and repair, reuse value and ultimate disposal.
3. A plan for preventive and predictive maintenance should be prepared for the equipment, and the estimated cost of maintenance and spare parts should be included in the economic analysis.

1.8 OBJECTIVES OF MATERIAL HANDLING

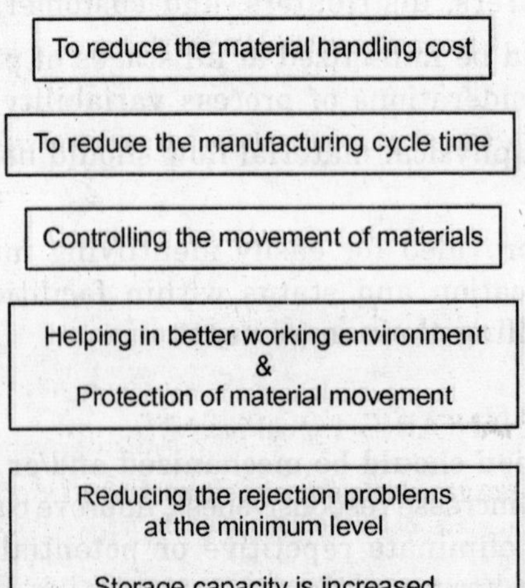

Fig. 1.3 Objectives of material handling

1.9 MATERIALS TRANSPORT SYSTEM

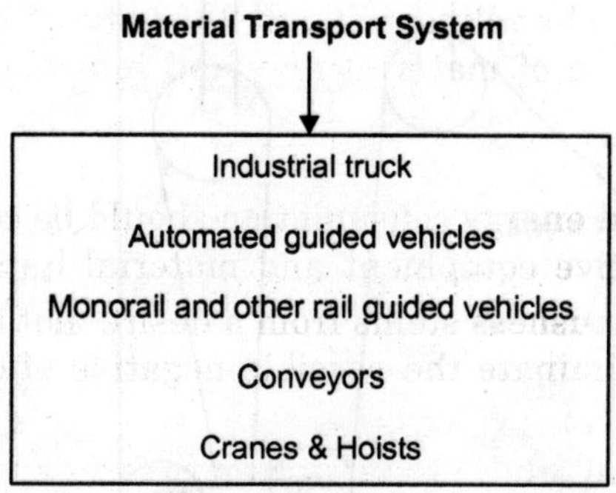

Fig. 1.5 Commonly used transport systems

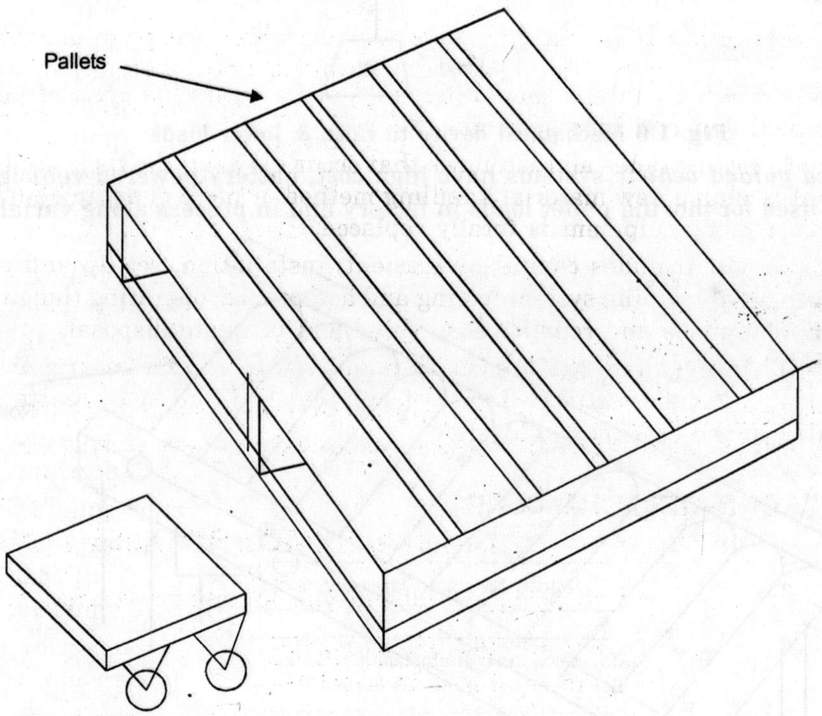

Fig. 1.5 (a)

1.10 FEATURES OF MATERIAL HANDLING EQUIPMENTS

Industrial trucks manual have low cost and low rate of delivery hours and can move only light loads in factory.

Industrial trucks powered have medium cost and can be used for movement of pallet loads and palletized containers in a factory or warehouse.

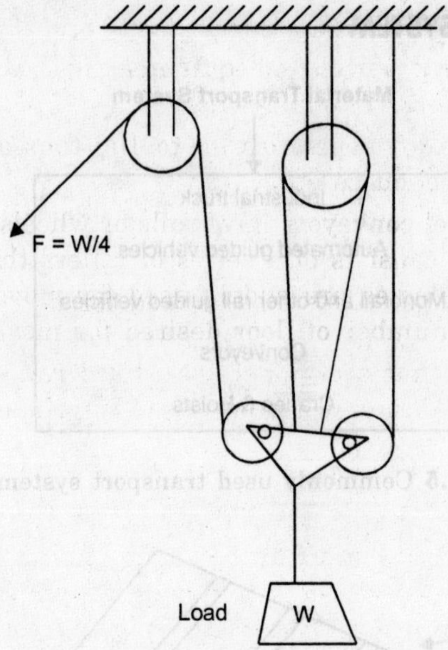

Fig. 1.6 Mechanical device to raise & lower loads

Automated guided vehicle systems have high cost, battery powered vehicles, flexible routing and is used for moving pallet loads in factory and in process along variable routes.

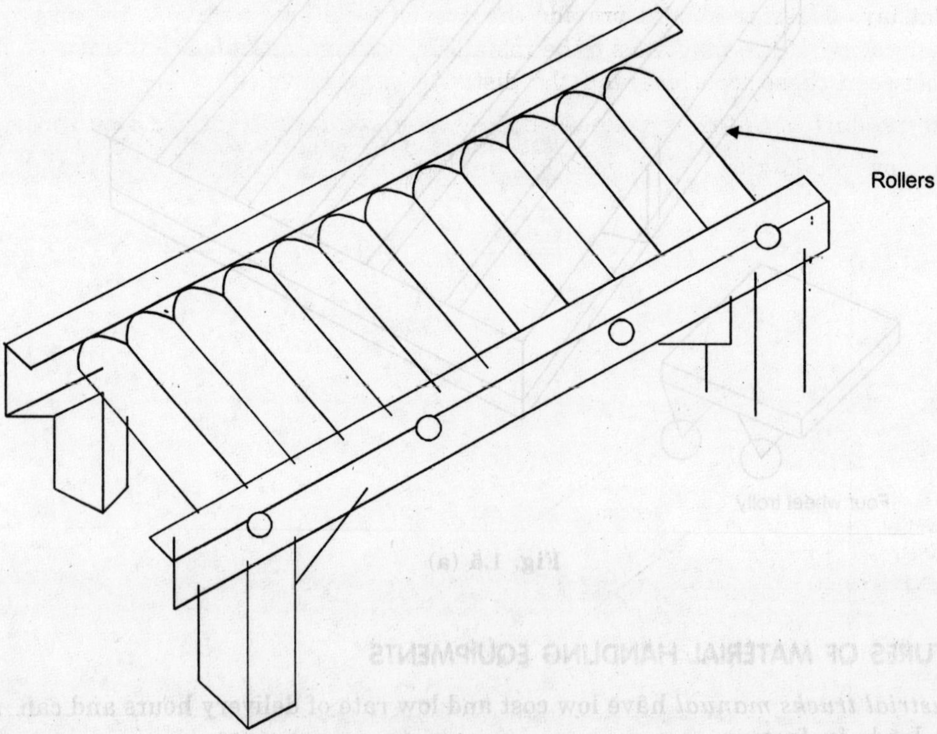

Fig. 1.7 Roller conveyor

Monorail or other guided systems have high cost, flexible routing and they move single\assemblies, products or pallet loads along variable routes in factory and can also move large quantity of materials.

Conveyors, powered great variety of equipment in floor, on the floor or overhead moving products along a manual assembly line.

Cranes and hoists have lift capacities up to 100 tons and they move large, heavy items in factories, mills, warehouses etc.

In roller and skate wheel conveyors have rolls or wheels on which the load rides. In roller conveyor the pathway consists of a series of rollers that are perpendicular to the direction level. These technologies are widely used for movement purpose just like lift moves from ground floor to number of floor desired for movement.

The motorized vehicles that are guided by a fixed rail system consist of either one rail or two parallel rails. Monorails in factories and warehouses are suspended overhead from the sealing.

Plant Layout

The layout of plant is very important before installing machines in production hall as the overall efficiency can be increased by reducing the material movement in production hall. All the machines planning is to be done by going through the type of processes desired and sequence of operation. The plant layout is to be made as the time and motion study can help in reducing the movement cost. In the case of a new establishment, the design of the handling system should be considered as part of the layout design. In the case of an existing facility, there is less flexibility in the design of the handling system. The plant layout design should provide the data of total area available in the production hall, the location of the machines to be installed, loading and unloading stations, possible routes between these locations and the distance to be traveled.

The product quantities produced in a factory can be categorized into three ranges:

1. Low production 2. Medium production 3. High production

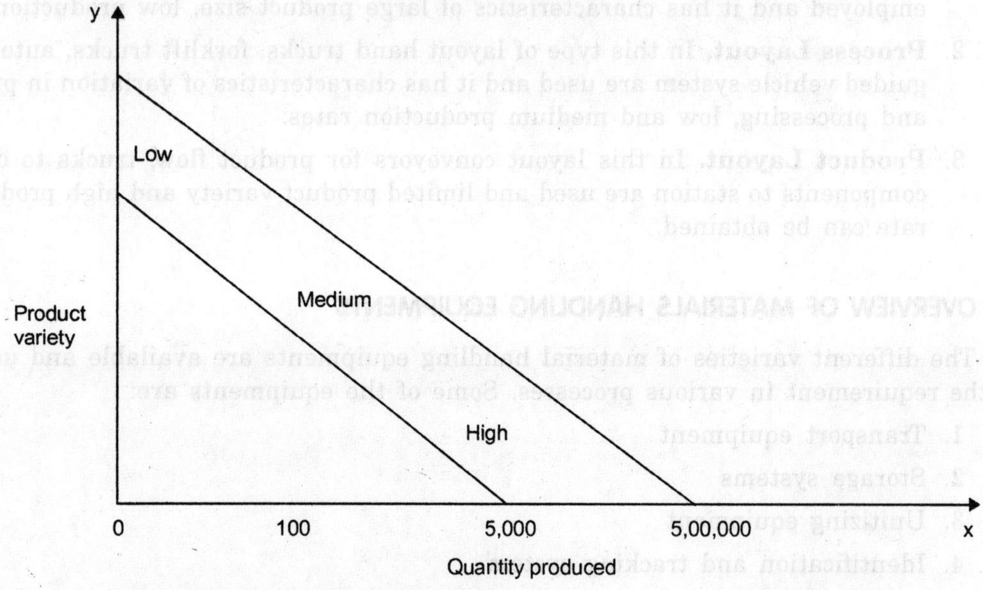

Fig. 1.8 Production variety and production quality relationship

Production Types

1. Job shop production
2. Batch production
3. Mass production.

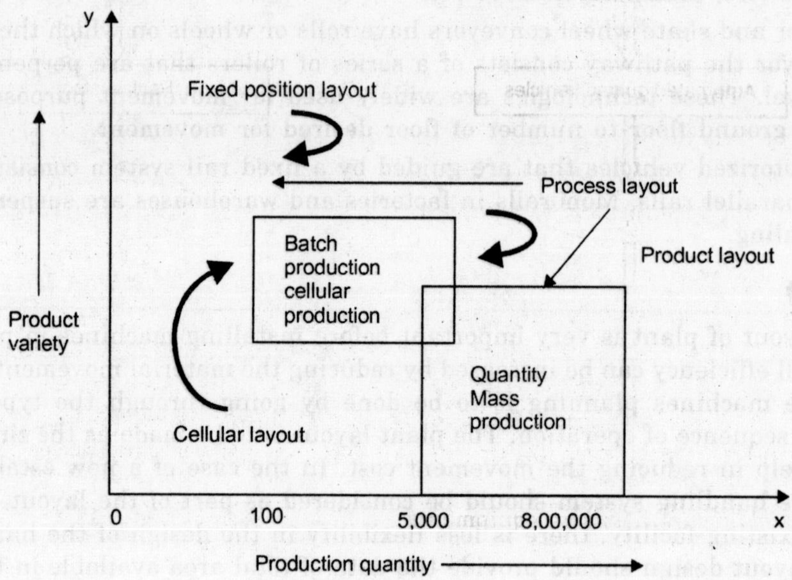

Fig. 1.9 Types of layout and facilities at different levels

Types of Material Handling Equipment Required for Different Layout

1. **Fixed Position Layout.** In this position cranes, hoists, industrial trucks are employed and it has characteristics of large product size, low production rate.
2. **Process Layout.** In this type of layout hand trucks, forklift trucks, automated guided vehicle system are used and it has characteristics of variation in product and processing, low and medium production rates.
3. **Product Layout.** In this layout conveyors for product flow, trucks to deliver components to station are used and limited product variety and high production rate can be obtained.

1.11 OVERVIEW OF MATERIALS HANDLING EQUIPMENTS

The different varieties of material handling equipments are available and used as per the requirement in various processes. Some of the equipments are:

1. Transport equipment
2. Storage systems
3. Unitizing equipment
4. Identification and tracking system.

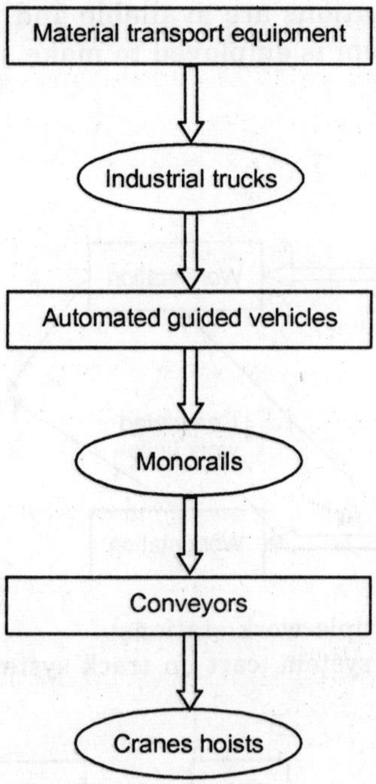

Fig. 1.10 Material handling equipments

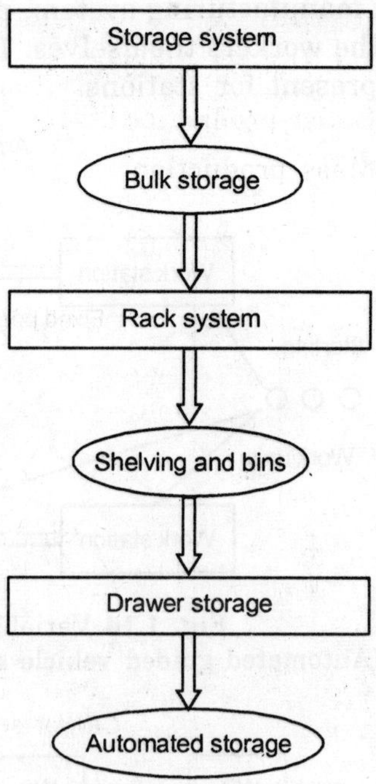

Fig. 1.11

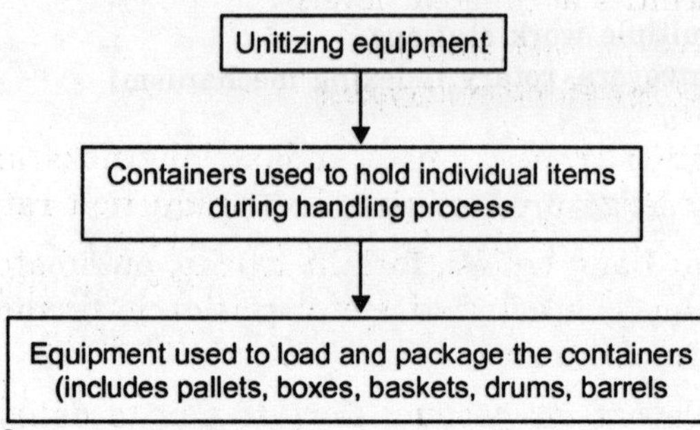

Fig. 1.12 Unitizing equipments

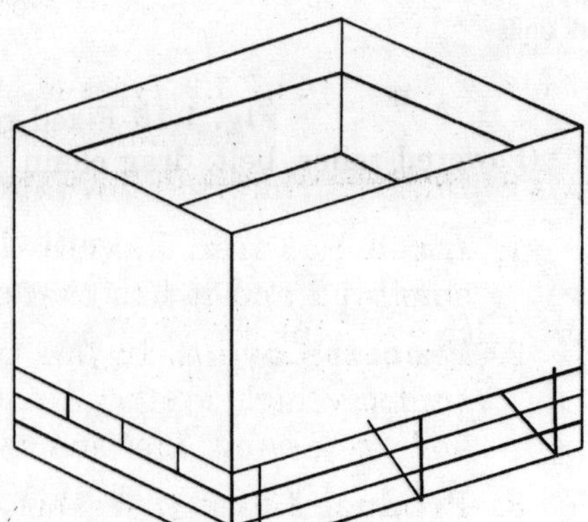

Fig. 1.13 Pallet box

1.12 MATERIALS HANDLING SYSTEM

In material handling system the functions in the processing and operation performed are:

1. Loading and unloading work units
2. Positioning the work units at each station
3. Transporting work units between stations
4. Temporary storage function.

As in manufacturing system, multiple work stations are available and the units are moved by the workers themselves. The storage system is employed to make sure the work is always present for stations.

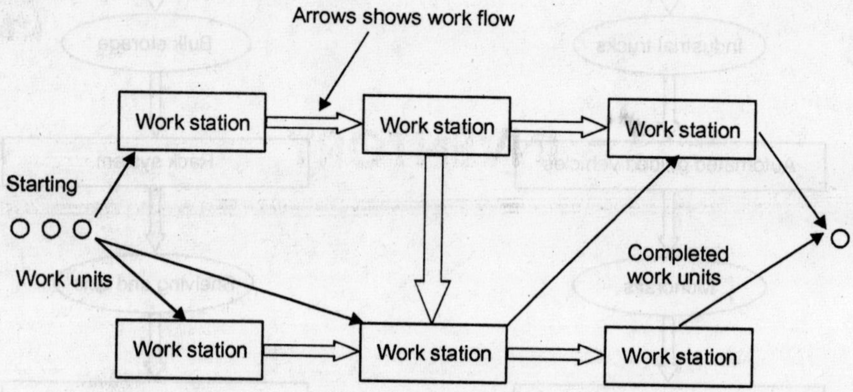

Fig. 1.14 Variable routing in multiple work stations
(Automated guided vehicle system, monorail system, cart on track system)

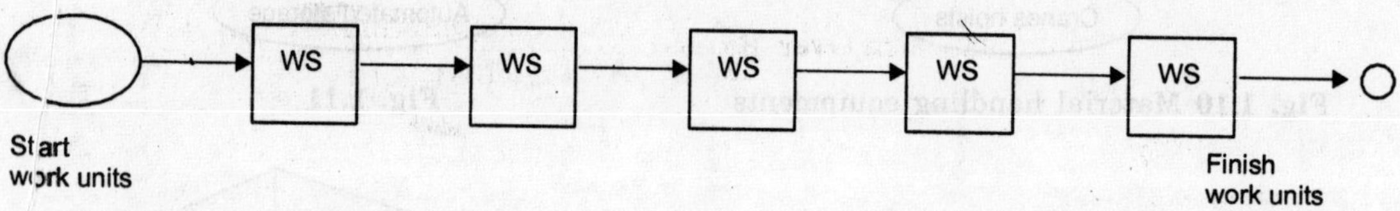

Fig. 1.15 Fixed routing in multiple work stations
(Powered roller, belt, drag chain, overhead conveyors, rotary indexing mechanism)

2

CHAPTER

INVENTORY

2.1 INTRODUCTION

From resource management point of view inventory can be termed as usable but idle resource.

Inventories can be taken as an index of materials management effectiveness.

$$\text{Inventory Turn Over Ratio} = \frac{\text{Total Consumption}}{\text{Average Inventory}}$$

Kinds of Inventory

1. Raw material.
2. Work in progress.
3. Finished goods.
4. Maintenance repair, and
5. Operating supplies spares inventory.

Higher the inventory turnover ratio the better is the way of reflection. Timely evaluation of the material is must. All forms of inventory are usable but idle resource if blocked money in a non productive opportunity cost in blocking the money.

Arrival inspection—Recording issue.

Purchasing disposal—Inventory control.

Indicators of Low Material Productivity

1. Excessive inventory or low inventory turnover ratio.
2. Long and uncertain replenishment lead time.
3. Large proportion of non moving (dead) in stock.
4. Excessive material handling/transportation cost.
5. Spoilage, scrap or waste of material.
6. Delays in meeting requirement.
7. Long retrieval and issue time in store.

8. Poor storage methods.
9. Buying from wrong source.
10. Excessive purchasing bill.
11. Too much variety of parts, lack of standardization.
12. Lack of material codification.
13. Long and inefficient purchase procedure.
14. Poor records keeping.
15. Quality problems for incoming materials. Inventory turnover ratio can be a good indicator of materials management's effectiveness and to control inventory we have to look at total system costs-both visible and hidden.

Possible Reasons for Low Material Production

1. **Lack of integrated system approach**—Different functional managers tend to look at materials-related decisions from their own narrow segmented sub system view point. For instance, production manager may want to minimize stock out while finance manager may like to minimize inventories. Many material management problems may be due to designers prescribing costlier material with too much variety and non standard dimensions.

   S.O.S—Surplus Obsolete and Scrap material. Every time handling is not good, it may affect the cost.

   Long retrieval—Poor storage functions as lot of items deal in storage that is location problem due to unable to locate the item. There is no standard code cut down waiting for improving the system.

2. In decision making related to materials, ignoring invisible (hidden) cost in preference to visible costs.

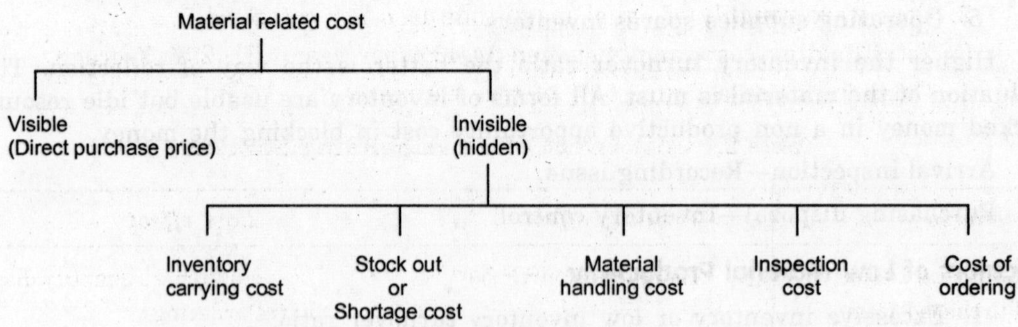

Fig. 2.1

We should look at total system cost both visible and hidden.

3. Uncertain supply/demand environment. Just-in-case environment. Source of uncertainty could be demand lead time, inflation, non availability, quality problems etc. Just-in-case environment *a dependable source of supply can be a great asset to Materials Management functions*.

4. Lack of scientific decision making—Using models of inventory planning and control.

Categorized holding of cost component C1

I. **Capital cost**

II. **Storage cost**

A. Land.

B. Building (owned):

(*a*) Depreciation.

(*b*) Property tax.

(*c*) Insurance.

(*d*) Utilities.

(*e*) Leased.

III. **Service cost**

A—Assessment: 1. Inventory taxes, 2. Insurance,

B—Processing: 1. Material handling, 2. Physical Inventory.

IV. **Risk cost**

A. Obsolescence.

B. Shrinkage:

1. Pilferage.
2. Disappearance.
3. Damage.
4. Spoilage.
5. Devaluation of selling price.

Finding of survey on estimation of holding cost is:

1. Capital cost is by far the most significant component as a % holding cost 49.95%.
2. Cost were roughly of equal magnitude in other categories.
3. Total holding cost range between 14-43% per year with 29% average.
4. Companies use a figure 50% of true estimate..

Table 2.1 Cost effect of an Impending Shortage

Scenario	*Primary effect*	*Cost effect*
*Remedial action Purchased item	Emergency purchase	Loss of purchase quantity discount Extra ordering Rush shipment
	Use of Substitute item	Higher cost/unit Adaptation cost Depletión of substitute item
*Remedial action manufactured item	Overtime	Premium labor rate Shift premium
	Sub contracting	Higher manufacturing cost
	Emergency hiring	Inefficient labor Risk of inferior-quality work

		Extra training expense
	Substitute item	Adaptation
		Higher unit cost
No remedial action	Lost Sale	Lost contribution
External demand	Lost customer	Additional contribution
	Additional lost customers	Additional contribution
	Backlogged demand	Goodwill loss
		Special delivery when item arrive
		Contract penalty
		Lawsuit
		Extra paper work.
No remedial action	Production downtime	Idle labor
Internal demand		Idle equipment
	Failure to see schedule	Eventually, see external demand
		Cost effects
	Unsafe condition	Damages

Table 2.2 Ordering Cost Categorization

Method of procurement	*Occasion*	*Ordering cost*
Purchase	Order approval	Paper work
	Order placement	Postage, phone charges
		Paper work
	Shipment	Freight
		Postage
		Demurrage
		Pickup
	Receipt of order	Identification and count verification
		Material handling
		Paper work
	Incoming inspection	Labour
		Paper work
	Billing	Paper work
Manufacture	Material receipt	Material handling
		Material
	Setup	Labor
		Overhead
	Shut down	Labor
		Material
		Overhead and Paper work
		Paper work

Ordering cost may have fixed and variable components. Variable cost may be included in the unit material cost. Only fixed component of ordering cost is taken for the purpose of optimization of inventory policy parameters.

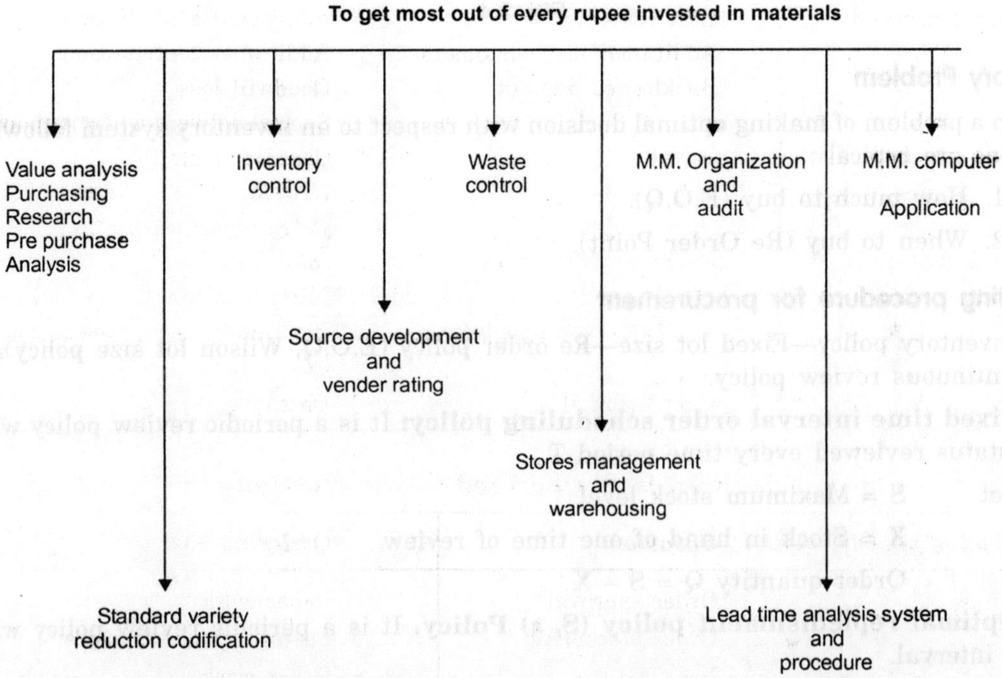

Fig. 2.2 Integrated system approach to materials management

2.2 INVENTORY MANAGEMENT

Inventory — Usable but idle resource with economic value.
— Raw material.
— Process inventory (work in process).
— Finished goods inventory.
— Maintenance repair and operating supplies.

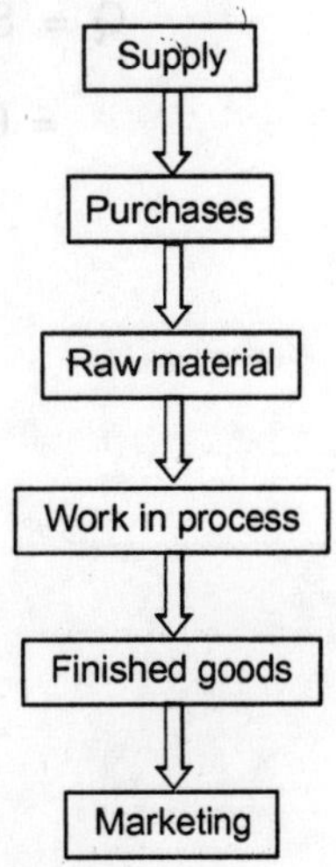

Fig. 2.3 Inventory Model—Representation of Reality

Inventory is needed because of (Time lapse/uncertainty) as while placing an order and receiving the material time is required i.e., the time lapse or lead time and to meet uncertainty of demand inventory is required.

Why inventory is required:

* Price inflation.
* Uncertainty of demand and supply.
* Extra transport cost must be minimized—fixed cost vs. variable cost—for economy of scale.

Fig. 2.4

Inventory Problem

In a problem of making optimal decision with respect to an inventory system following decisions are typical :

1. How much to buy (E.O.Q).
2. When to buy (Re Order Point).

Operating procedure for procurement

Inventory policy—Fixed lot size—Re order policy (E.O.Q, Wilson lot size policy). It is a continuous review policy.

Fixed time interval order scheduling policy: It is a periodic review policy with stock status reviewed every time period T.

Let S = Maximum stock level

X = Stock in hand of one time of review

Order quantity Q = S – X

Optimal replenisnment policy (S, *s*) Policy. It is a periodic review policy with *v* time interval.

S = Maximum stock level

s = Minimum stock level

X = Stock in hand at the time of review

$$Q = S - X, \; x \leq s$$
$$= 0, \; x \leq s$$

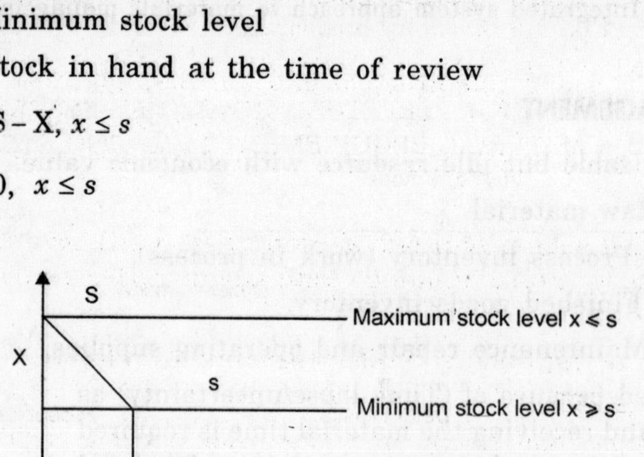

Fig. 2.5

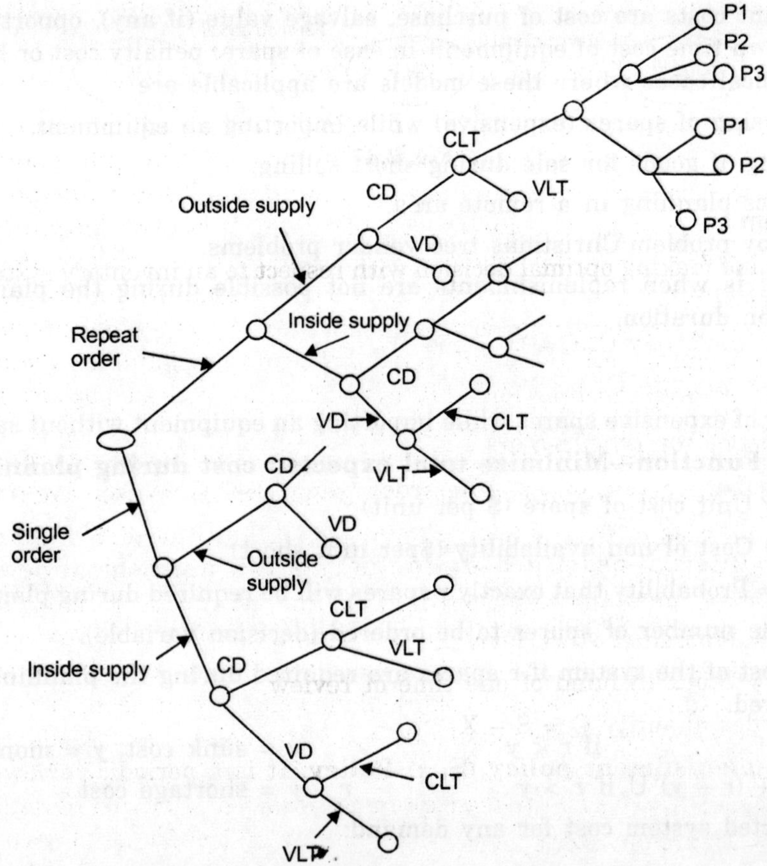

Fig. 2.6 Inventory problem classification

CD = CONSTANT DEMAND, VD = VARIABLE DEMAND, CLT = CONSTANT LEAD TIME VLT = VARIABLE LEAD TIME, P1 = PERPETUAL INVENTORY SYSTEM, P2 = PERIODIC INVENTORY SYSTEM, P3 = MATERIAL REQUIREMENT PLANNING SYSTEM.

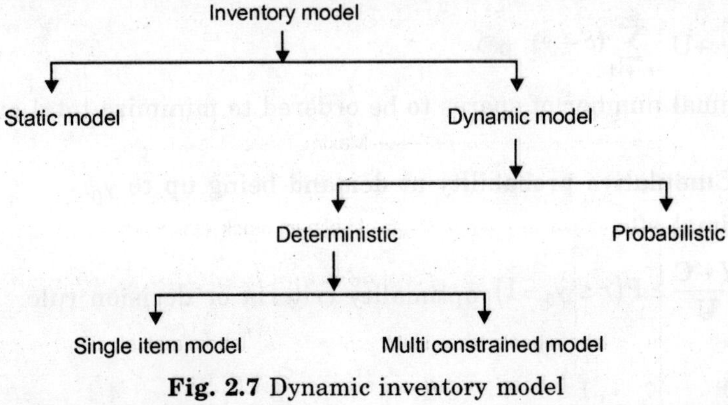

Fig. 2.7 Dynamic inventory model

2.3 STATIC INVENTORY MODELS

These are single purchase decision models for a single period without replenishments. It is a kind of type (1, 2) model where balancing of cost is to be done between cost of having and cost of not having an item on stock. Only how much to buy is relevant decision variable. Relevant costs are cost of purchase, salvage value (if any), opportunity cost of shortage like down time cost of equipment(in case of spare) penalty cost or lost potential profit. Some typical cases where these models are applicable are :

1. Purchasing of spares (expensive) while importing an equipment.
2. Stocking of goods for sale during short selling.
3. Logistics planning in a remote area.
4. Newsboy problem/Christmas tree vendor problems.

Simple test is when replenishments are not possible during the planning period project or mission duration.

Model-1

Purchasing of expensive spares while importing an equipment without salvage value.

Objective Function—Minimize total expected cost during planning period.

Let C = Unit cost of spare ($ per unit)

U = Cost of non availability ($per unit short)

P® = Probability that exactly r spares will be required during planning period.

Let y be the number of spares to be ordered (decision variable).

If Cry = Cost of the system if r spares are required during the planning period but only y are ordered.

Cry = cy if $r < y$ c = sunk cost, y = money invested

= $c.y + (r - y)$ U if $r > y$ $r - y$ = shortage cost

Total expected system cost for any demand:

$$\Sigma\,(\text{Cry}) = \sum_{0}^{\infty} \text{cry}\ .\text{P®}$$

$$= \sum_{r=0}^{\infty} \text{cry}\ .\text{P®} + \sum_{r=y+1}^{\infty} (c - y + (r - y)u)\ .\text{p®}$$

$$= cy + \text{U} \sum_{r=y+1}^{\infty} (c - y)\ \text{p®}$$

Let Y_0 = Optimal number of spares to be ordered to minimize total expected system cost E (cry).

$P(r \geq y_0)$ = Cumulative probability at demand being up to y_0.

Then. for optimal $y0$,

$$P(r \leq y_0) \geq \frac{\text{Y} - \text{C}}{\text{U}} \geq P(r \leq y_0 - 1)$$ optimality criteria or decision rule.

Example:

R	0	1	2	3	4	5	6
P®	0.923	0.04	0.02	0.01	0.005	0.002	0

U = $10,000,000

C = $100,000

$P(r < y)$ = E P®	0.923	0.963	0.983	0.993	0.998	1.0	1.0

$$\frac{Y-C}{U} = 0.99 \Rightarrow y_0 3$$

Risk of shortage = 0.99 = 0.01

Model–2

When spare has salvage value =V

$$\text{Cry} = c.\ y - (y - r)\ v \qquad \text{if } r < y$$
$$= c.\ y + (r - y)\ u \qquad \text{if } r > y$$

$$E(\text{Cry}) = (c.\ y) + u \sum_{r=y+1}^{\infty} (r - y)\ p® \ -v \sum_{0}^{y} (r - y)\ .p\ ®$$

Optimality criteria— $P(r \le y_0) \ge \frac{u-c}{u-v} \ge P(r \le y_0 - 1)$

If V = 0, it is same as model 1

Example—*c, v* and P ® same as example of model 1 and v = $ 50,000

Sol: $u\text{–}c/u\text{–}v = 0.998$ $\qquad y_0 = 4$

Dynamic Inventory Models
Repetitive purchase (Replenishment decisions)

Majority of inventory problems belong to this class of decision situation in real life when one has to make replenishment decisions on an ongoing basis over time concerning consumable materials spares etc.

Miller and Starr call this group of models as dynamic inventory models.

Key questions: 1. **How much to replenish?**

(Order Size)

2. **When to replenish (order timings)**

Selection of an appropriate inventory Policy

Before we develop/choose an inventory model for optimization of decision variables in order to minimizes TSC (Total System Cost), we should decide on the appropriate inventory policy to be followed. Some common policies to choose from are:

1. **Lot Size (E.O.Q) Policy:** Inventory is continuously reviewed: lot size Q and reorder point R are two decision variables.
2. **Order Level Policy:** Inventory status reviewed every T periods: max stock level is. s, S, T are the decision variables. Order size may vary from period to period.
3. **Optional Replenishment (s, S) Policy:** Stock level is reviewed every T periods. Max stock level S, Min stock level s are decision variables. S, s, T are all decision variables.

Just in Time Production System

JIT production systems were developed in Japan to minimize inventories especially WIP. WIP and other types of inventory are seen by Japanese as waste that should be minimized or eliminated. The ideal Just in Time production system produces and delivers exactly the required number of each component to the downstream operation in the manufacturing sequence just at the time when that component is needed. Each component is delivered just in time. This delivery discipline minimizes WIP and manufacturing lead time as well as the space and money invested in WIP. The JIT discipline can be applied not only to production operation but to supplier delivery operations as well. The JIT production discipline has shown itself to be very effective in high volume repetitive operations, such as those found in automotive industry.

2.4 ABC ANALYSIS (Total Cumulative Cost vs.% of items)

ABC Analysis—In this method the materials are classified in to three categories costly items which are 10 to 20% of the total items and may aeeowe for about 50% of the total value of the stores. As more finance is invalid in a category therefore more attention to he given. Group B consists of items which constitute 20 to 30% of the store items and represents about 30% of the total value of stores. In group C about 70 is 80% of the items are covered costing about 20% of the total value. Procedure of ABC analysis:

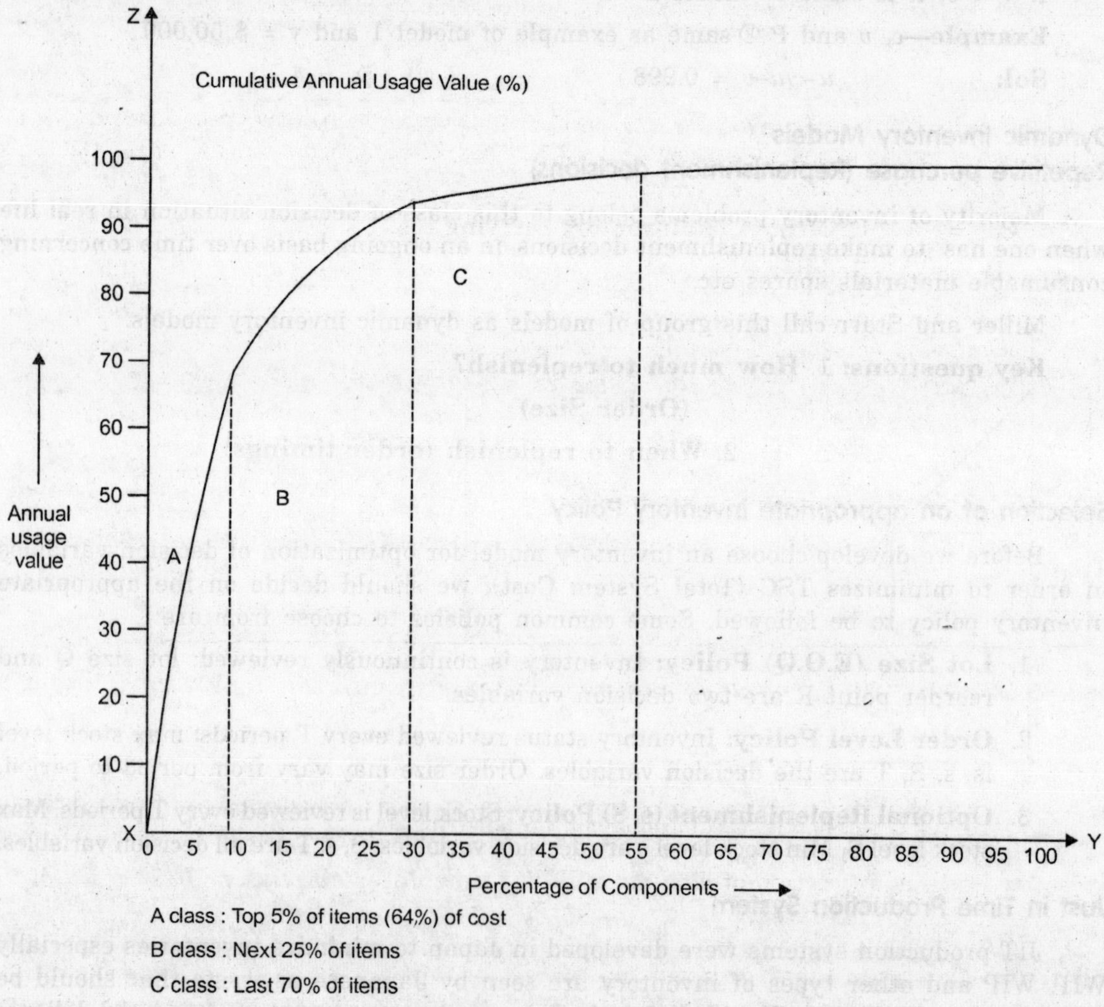

Fig. 2.8 : ABC (Analysis)

1. Identify all the items used in an organisahan.
2. List all the items as per their values.
3. Court the number of items and categorise value wise i.e., high value, Medium value and low value etc.
4. Find the Percentage of all items i.e., high, medium and low valued items of total inventory cost.
5. Plot a graph of percentage of components vs Annual usage value.

FSN-ABC-VED Analysis

First group items into: Fast moving (Regular consumption)

FSN Categories **Slow Moving**

Non Moving

For fast moving items conventional inventory models of EOQ/Fixed interval scheduling etc. may be applicable. ABS-VED analysis is useful to identify items requiring rigorous control.

(Q,R) Policy for A class items.

$$Q = \sqrt{\frac{2rc_3}{c_1}} = EOQ$$

C3 = Ordering Cost/Inventory carrying cost

R = Reorder Point

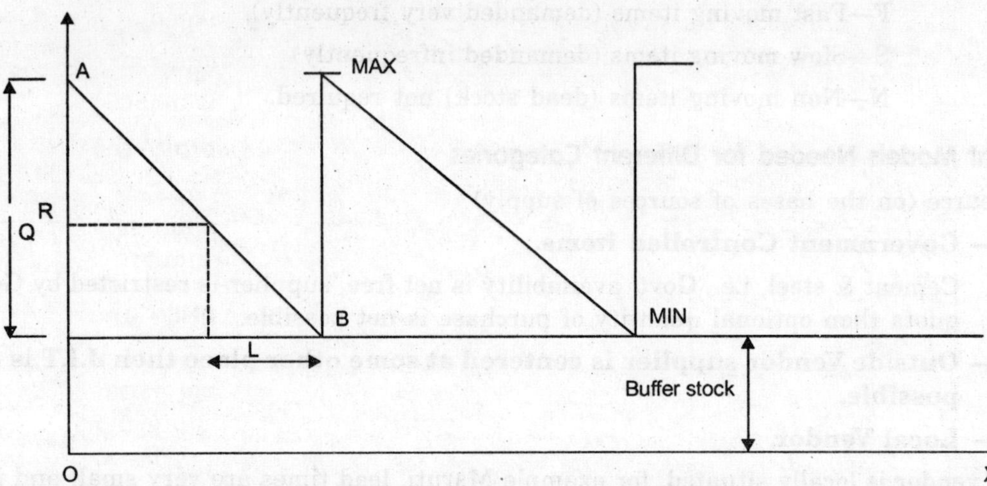

Fig. 2.9 Paretos lam of indistribution

Buffer Stock is a function of demand and lead time uncertainty as well as % risk of shortage that can be tolerated.

V-E-D Analysis

In group items units.

Vital— (must have in stock when needed) Items on critical path.

Essential— (should have) On Sub critical path.

Desirable— (can have) On non-critical path.

The analysis is based on the cost of shortage basis for vital items. Cost of shortage is very high and it is of vital importance to have the item in stock when demanded. For essential items it is lower than vital. For desirable items it is not very high.

Table 2.3 Two Way Classification and Policy on Service Level

	V	E	D
A	95	80	50
B	99.5	90	75
C	99.99	95	90

→ **Service level aimed** at for various categories (only for illustration)

Movement Analysis: F-S-N Analysis depending upon frequency of demands

F—Fast moving items (demanded very frequently)

S—Slow moving items (demanded infrequently)

N—Non moving items (dead stock) not required.

Different Models Needed for Different Categories

Source (on the bases of sources of supply)

G — Government Controlled items.

Cement & steel, i.e., Govt. availability is not free, supplier is restricted by Govt. quota then optional quantity of purchase is not possible.

O — Outside Vendor supplier is centered at some other place then J.I.T is not possible.

L — Local Vendor.

If vendor is locally situated, for example Maruti, lead times are very small and it is possible to have multiple item purchase.

Foreign Source of supply

In Maruti 1/3rd components come from Japan and therefore greater lead time is involved. Greater procedures are required. Nature and location are important.

Certain materials are in **dead stock**. If we know that the material have been lying for the last five years then find out what can be done, that is then stop the procurement, proceed in disposal of items.

XYZ 100% of items non moving then how to select kind of ABC analysis in dead stock.

Value of Material = Numbers of items × Unit Price, that is value of dead stock is kind of selective focus. Focuses 10% of the items which has value of 5 lakh.

2.5 HOW JIT MINIMIZES PRODUCTION LEAD TIME

In order to minimize production lead time spent by incoming material from suppliers prior to processing, the actual processing time and the time spent by outgoing material prior to delivery to customers, following steps should be taken:

For Incoming Material

1. Do not inspect,
2. Do not store,
3. Have delivered directly to the production process,
4. Minimize paper work,
5. Order the amounts to be processed per period.

For Actual Processing

1. Do not inspect,
2. Do not rework,
3. Minimize process flow distance,
4. Minimize set-up time,
5. Minimize lot size,
6. Operate in minimum work in process,
7. Minimize paper work,
8. Do not produce extra units.

For Outgoing Material

1. Do not store,
2. Do not inspect,
3. Ship only perfect units,
4. Minimize paper work.

JIT Deliveries

Frequent and in small lots and eliminate the need for storage and provide the right amount for processing.

Dock to line deliveries will provide material movement directly to processing.

Monthly statement, computer transactions or kanban will minimize paper work.

For Actual Processing

Quality at the source, statistical process control and mistake proofing will eliminate rework and inspection as separate activities.

Dedicated lines and flow layouts will minimize process flow distances.

SMED (Single minute exchange of die) will cut set-up times and allow for reduced lot sizes and minimum work in process.

Kanban will minimize paper work.

Pull system, matching production to demand will eliminate time wasted on producing extra units prior to the time they are needed.

For Outgoing Material

Quality at the source, statistical process control and mistake proofing in the production process will minimize any requirement for inspection prior to shipping and ensure quality in shipped units.

2.6 AGGREGATE INVENTORY ANALYSIS (Exchange curve or optimal policy curve concept)

Aggregate inventory analysis enables us to examine the rationality of existing procurement policies at the macro level in the organization. It can be used to quickly detect if our present procurement practices are rationalized and if so, how much potential for inventory reduction exists. Optimal Policy curve (Starr & Miller) on Exchange curve (Peterson & Silver) concept is very useful for such purpose.

Concept: A rational procurement policy is one which attains an appropriate trade-off between carrying cost and ordering cost. Thus a rational policy will aim at minimizing total inventory held for a stated level of procurement efforts or will allow minimizing number of orders for a given inventory level.

If TCS = Total cycle stock (inventory) in $ per year

N = Total number of orders per year

Qi = Order quantity of ith item

Di = Annual demand for ith item

Vi = unit price for ith item;$/unit

Prob. 1 Minimize TCS = $\frac{1}{2}\Sigma QiVi$ subject to summation of $\Sigma Di/Qi$ = N (given)

Prob. 2 Minimize N = ? of $\Sigma Di/Qi$ subject to summation of $\Sigma\frac{Qi\,Vi}{2}$ = TCS (given)

Solving these problems as constrained optimization problems; the characteristics of optimal policy

$$(TCS)\ N = \text{constant} = k = \frac{1}{2}\left(\Sigma\sqrt{Di\,Vi}\right)^2$$ of under root Di.Vi whole square

$$\frac{TCS}{N} = \frac{C_3}{i}$$ where C_3 = ordering cost/order and i = fraction of carrying cost

If C_3/i is warily constant for various items; then (TCS)N = K = constant; TCS/N = constant.

Relationship between TCS and N is a rectangular hyperbola and is called the exchange curve or the optimal policy curve if Di, Vi are known; the exchange curve can be plotted by computing k first.

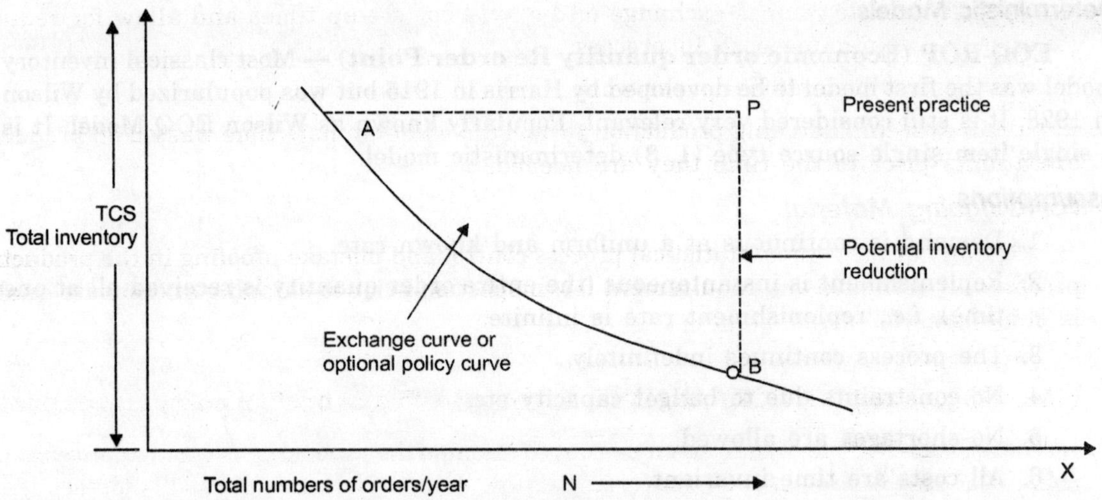

Fig. 2.10

How to Determine Rationality of Present Practice

After having plotted exchange curve, the present practice can be identified at point P if total cycle stock at present is estimated together with present number of procurement orders per year. If P is above exchange curve, it indicates departure from rational trade-off, hence the need for rationalization.

Potential for Inventory Reduction

If rationalization is done along path PB to minimize TCS for existing N, then distance PB indicates the potential for inventory reduction. If path PA is followed, then distance PA indicates reduction in ordering effort for given TCS.

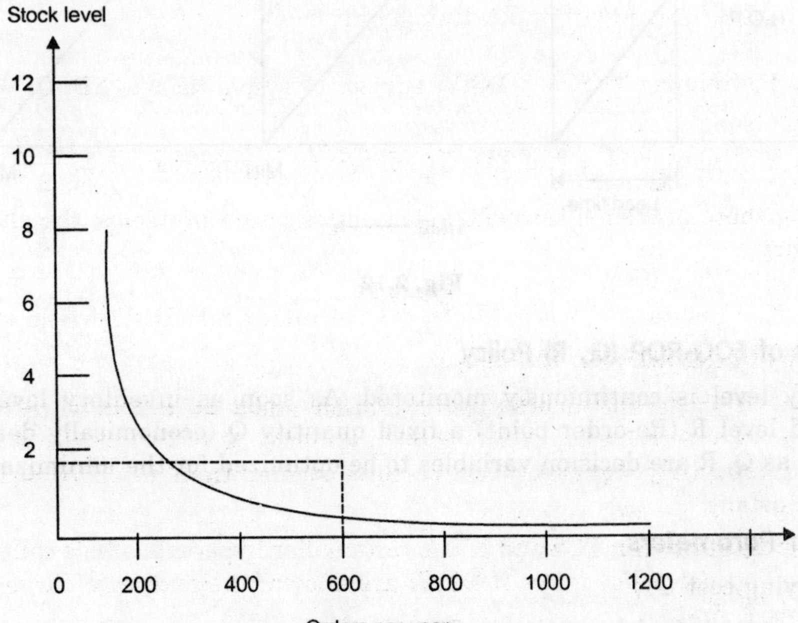

Fig. 2.11 Exchange curve

Deterministic Models

EOQ-ROP (Economic order quantity Re order Point) — Most classical inventory model was the first model to be developed by Harris in 1915 but was popularized by Wilson in 1928. It is still considered very relevant. Popularly known as Wilson EOQ Model. It is a single item single source type (1, 3) deteriministic model.

Assumptions

1. Demand is continuous at a uniform and known rate.
2. Replenishment is instantaneous (the entire order quantity is received all at one time), *i.e.,* replenishment rate is infinite.
3. The process continues indefinitely.
4. No constraints due to budget capacity etc.
5. No shortages are allowed.
6. All costs are time invariant.
7. Quantity discounts are not available.
8. Lead time is deterministic.
9. Inventory is continuously reviewed/monitored.

Inventory Graph

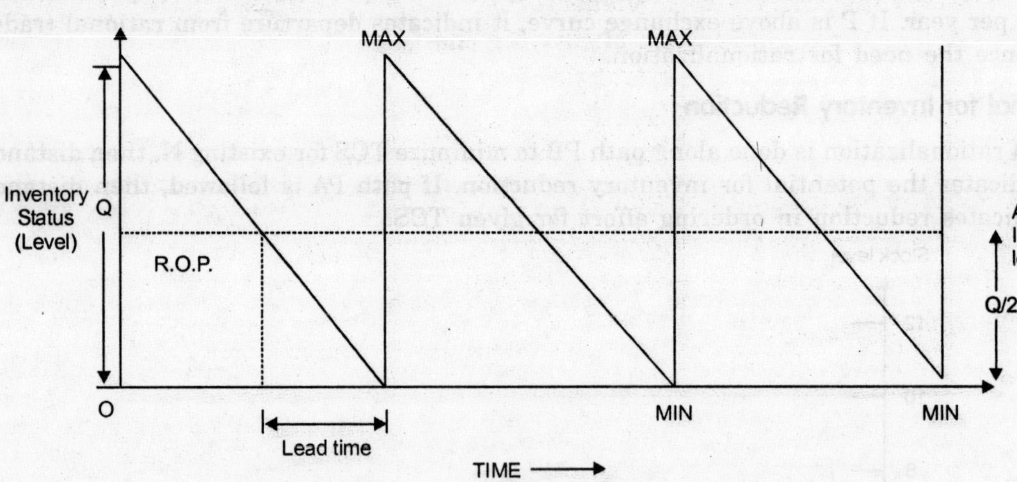

Fig. 2.12

Rating Aspect of EOQ-ROP (Q, R) Policy

Inventory level is continuously monitored. As soon as inventory level falls to a predetermined level R (Re-order point) a fixed quantity Q (economically determined) is ordered again as Q, R are decision variables to be optimized for the minimization of total system cost.

Relevant Cost Parameters

1. Carrying cost C1,
2. Ordering (replenishment) cost C3.

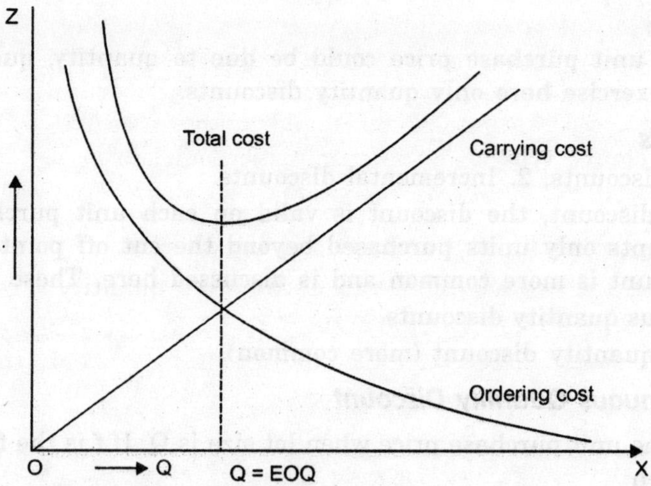

Fig. 2.13

Illustrations

Let R be the annual demand (units/yr)

C1 = Unit holding(carrying) cost \$/item/yr

C3 = Unit ordering cost (\$/order)

C1 = (I, P) if I = Fraction of carrying charge/yr.

P = Unit price(\$/unit)

TC = Total system cost(\$per year)

Analysis

Average inventory = Q/2

Total number of orders/yr = R/Q

Total system cost (TC) = C1.Q/2+C3.(R/Q)

Optimality Condition

$$\frac{\partial TC}{\partial Q} = 0;$$

$$\frac{\partial^2 C}{\partial Q2} = 2C3R/Q3 > 0$$

Hence total cost function is cover

$$EOQ = Q^* = \sqrt{2RC3/CI}$$

$$TC^* = \sqrt{2RC3/C3}$$

Determination of reorder point is straight forward.

2.7 INVENTORY MODELS WITH QUANTITY DISCOUNTS (PRICE BREAKS)

Many times in practice, suppliers offer quantity discounts as a sales promotion strategy to encourage bulk ordering of materials. If this is so, the total purchase bill is no longer constraint and is a function of decision variable. The decision model should include this.

Discounts

Reduction in unit purchase price could be due to quantity, quality, season, cash payment etc. We exercise here only quantity discounts.

Types of Discounts

1. All units discounts, 2. Incremental discounts.

In all units discount, the discount is valid on each unit purchased, whereas in incremental discounts only units purchased beyond the cut off points are on discount. First type of discount is more common and is discussed here. These are of two types:

1. Continuous quantity discounts
2. Discrete quantity discount (more common).

Model with Continuous Quantity Discount

Let b(Q) be the unit purchase price when lot size is Q. If f is the fraction of carrying cost/unit time, then

$$C1 = f.b(Q)$$

Replenishment cost now includes the visible cost of direct purchase bill.

$$C3' = C3 + Q.b(Q)$$

Total system cost expression is

$$\begin{aligned} TC(Q) &= f.b(Q).Q/2 + [\ C3 + Q.b(Q)]\ R/Q \\ &= 1/2\ f.\ b(Q).Q + C3.R/Q + R.b(Q) \end{aligned}$$

Solution of this depends upon the form of function b(Q).

Multi Echelon Inventory Systems

System structure—Stock distributed at various locations in the system to keep it nearer to the point of consumption. Multi echelon inventory (Multi stage) or multi level inventory problems are concerned with a variety of inventory problems involving supply of two or more interrelated production facilities.

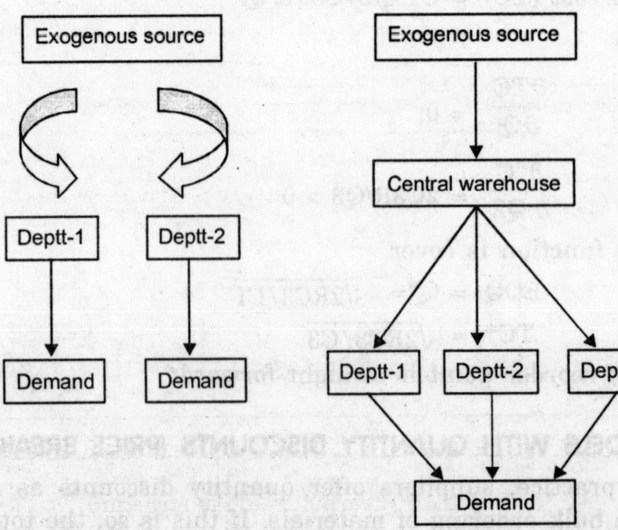

Fig. 2.14 Multi echelon inventory system structure

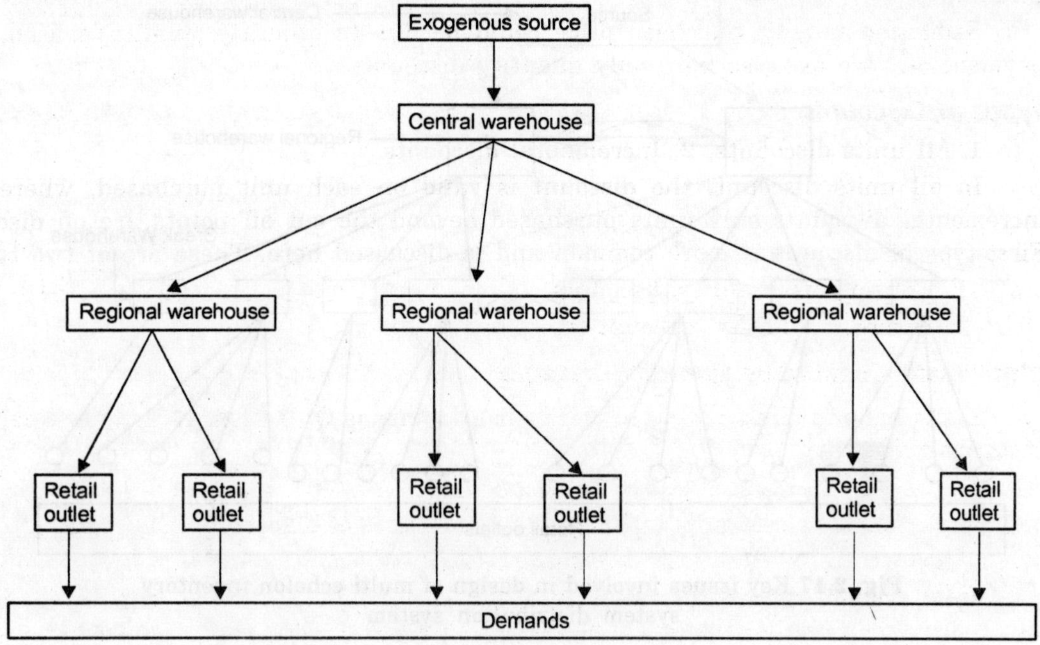

Fig. 2.15 System structure

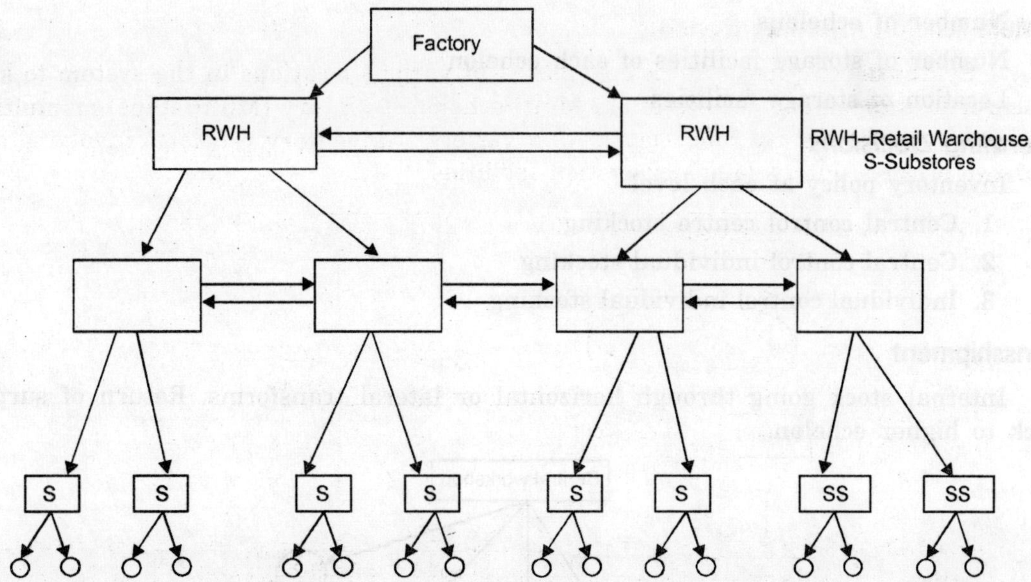

Fig. 2.16 Inverted tree like structure

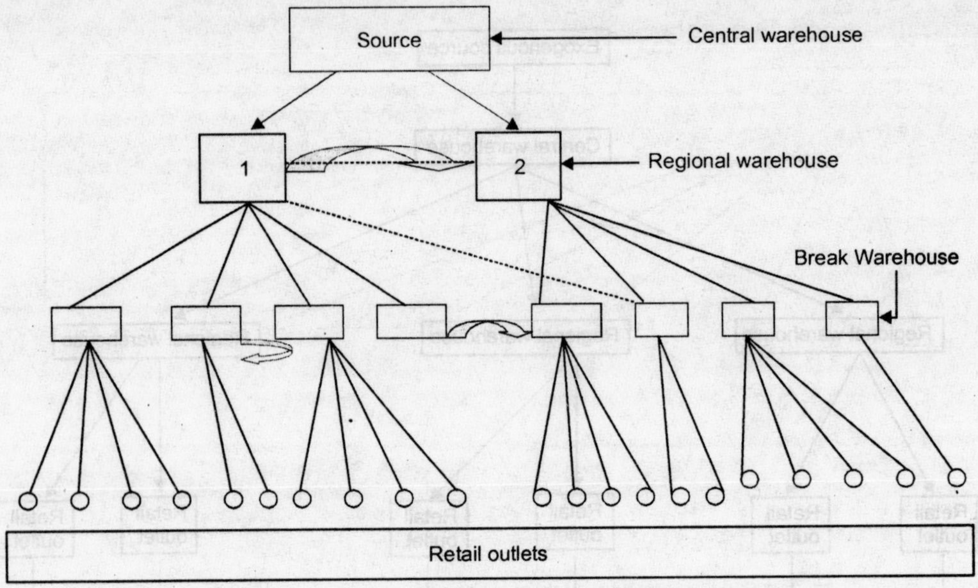

Fig. 2.17 Key issues involved in design of multi echelon inventory system distribution system

Strategic Decision in design of distribution network

Network

Number of echelons

Number of storage facilities of each echelon

Location of storage facilities

Operating Decisions

Inventory policy at each level

1. Central control centre stocking
2. Central control individual stocking
3. Individual control individual stocking

Transshipment

Internal stock going through horizontal or lateral transforms. Return of surplus stock to higher echelon.

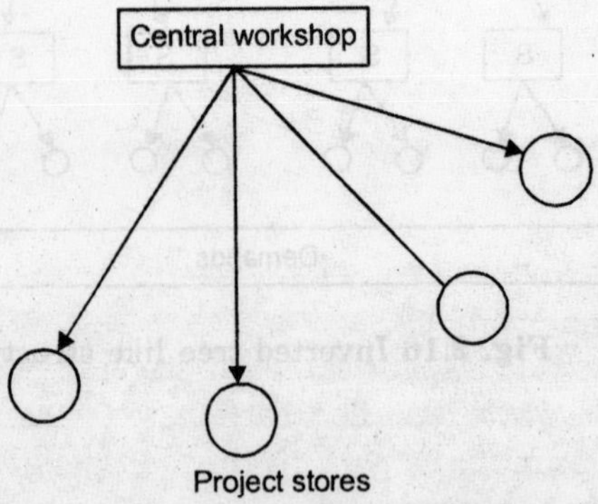

Individually demand is slow moving but when pulled up becomes fast moving.

Multi echelon Repair Inventory System

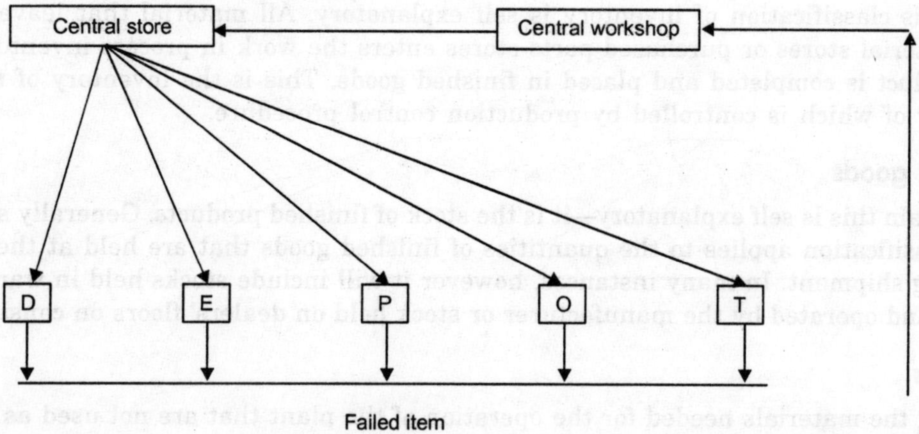

Fig. 2.18

Objective of Inventory Management and control

The ultimate objective of all manufacturing controls is to realize a profit through the operation of the business. A more restricted objective of the control of the material is to satisfy the customer by meeting the schedule for deliveries. Failure to deliver order on time is one principal cause for loss of business and customers. Effective control of the material throughout the manufacturing cycle prevents this problem from arising.

Specific objectives of the inventory management and control group are to maintain optimum inventory levels and inventory turnover for operation of the business at maximum profit—also through the control of inventories, to insure that the right material, in the right quantity and of right quality, is made available at the right place at the right time.

Inventory Classification

Much as we identify the various functions in materials management with the flow of goods, we can identify the different types of inventories or stock of material maintained in a manufacturing plant. All plants use the same general classification of inventories, including raw material, purchased parts, work in progress, finished goods and supplies.

Raw material

A raw material inventory includes all items that after being received at the plant require additional processing before becoming an identifiable part of the finished product of one plant—such as roll, bar and steel may be the raw material for the next industrial purchaser.

Purchased parts

This classification of inventory is applied to component part of a product that needs no additional processing before being assembled into the finished product. In some cases this material may be classified as raw material inventory. More often than not, however a separate classification is justified. The carburetor that is the finished product of one manufacturer becomes a purchased part to the automobile manufacturer.

Work in process

This classification of inventory is self explanatory. All material that leaves either raw material stores or purchased parts stores enters the work in process inventory until the product is completed and placed in finished goods. This is the inventory of material the flow of which is controlled by production control procedure.

Finished goods

Again this is self explanatory—it is the stock of finished products. Generally speaking this classification applies to the quantities of finished goods that are held at the factory awaiting shipment. In many instances, however it will include stocks held in warehouses owned and operated by the manufacturer or stock held on dealers' floors on consignment.

Supplies

All the materials needed for the operation of the plant that are not used as parts of the finished product are classified as supplies. The material that becomes part of the finished product is called direct material. Lubricating oils, sweeping compound, light bulbs, and many other items fall into the supply category.

Inventory Management

The planning of the control of inventory can be divided into two phases:

INVENTORY MANAGEMENT
INVENTORY CONTROL

Inventory management accomplishes the first phase, consisting of:

- Determination of the degree of control that is required for the best results
- Determination of optimum inventory levels and procedures for their review and adjustment
- Planning and design of the inventory control system
- Planning of the inventory control organization

The second phase of planning, which is the day-to-day planning required to meet production requirements, we shall discuss later as inventory control.

Inventory Controls

The inventory control group puts the plans of inventory management into operation. These plans are seldom complete in every detail. The day to day planning required to meet production requirements—the second phase of planning for inventory control—is the responsibility of inventory control group. Another responsibility is the recording and reporting of transactions involving movement of materials and of the effect on the different inventories. This is the picture of actual accomplishment by the plant of the flow of material. The comparison of this performance to the existing inventory plan, and the evaluation of the current material control situation, together comprise the next step in inventory control. The most important step, however, is the initiation of corrective actions. As we have indicated before, modern manufacturing requires careful planning.

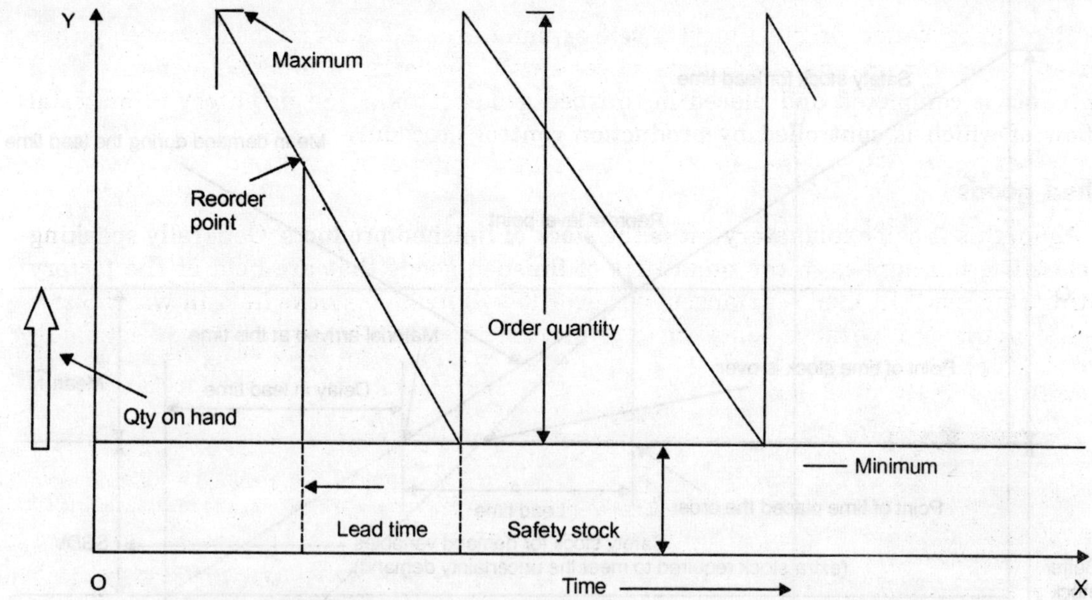

Fig. 2.19 Constant usage and instant replacement inventory model

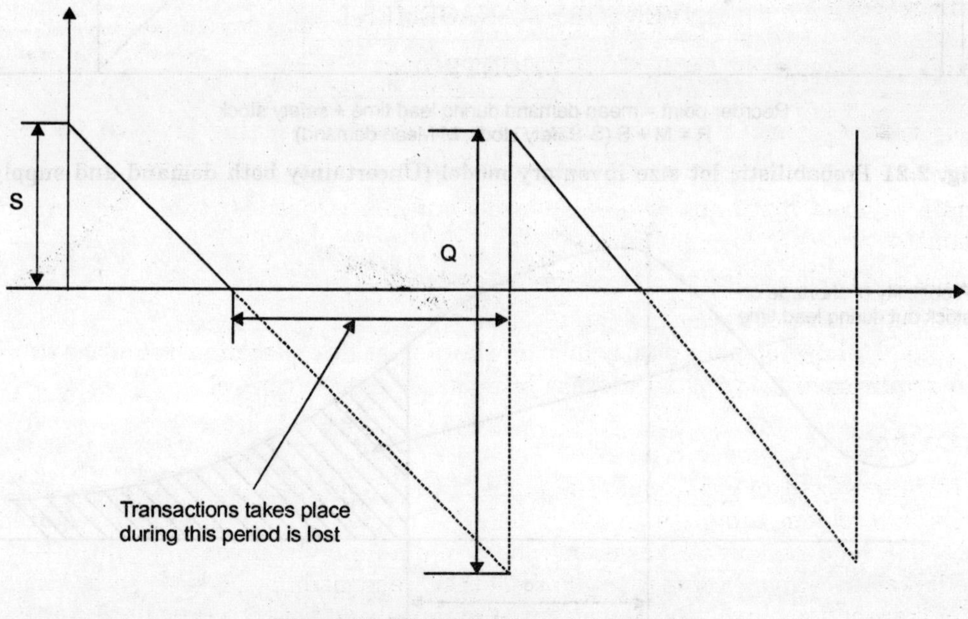

Fig. 2.20 EOQ model with lost sales

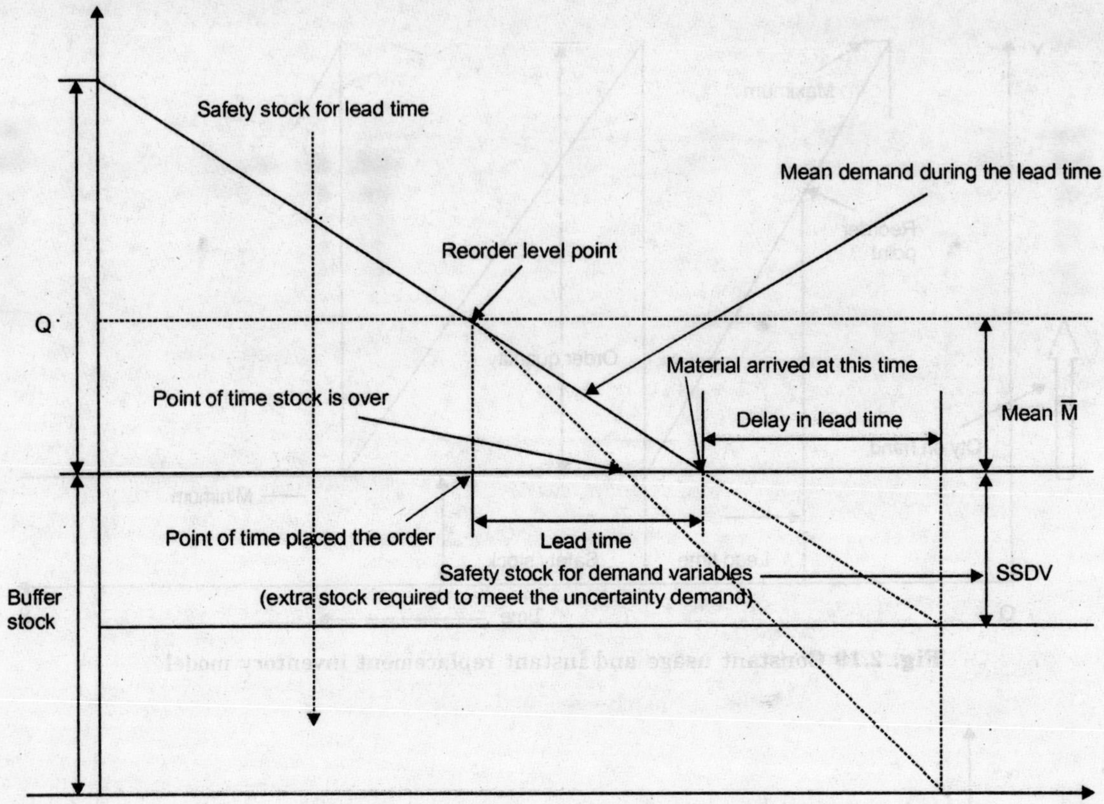

Reorder point = mean demand during lead time + safety stock
R = M + S (S-Safety stock, M-Mean demand)

Fig. 2.21 Probabilistic lot size inventory model (Uncertainty both demand and supply)

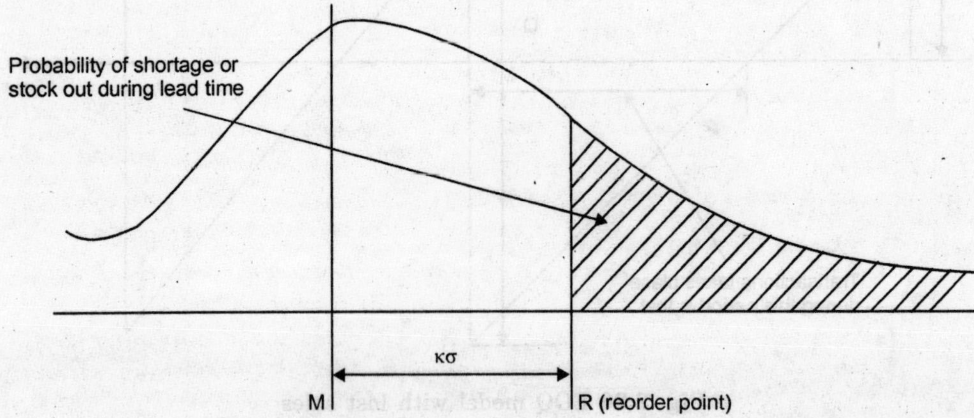

(Mean time during the lead time)

S = safety stock
σ = standard deviation of lead time

Fig. 2.22

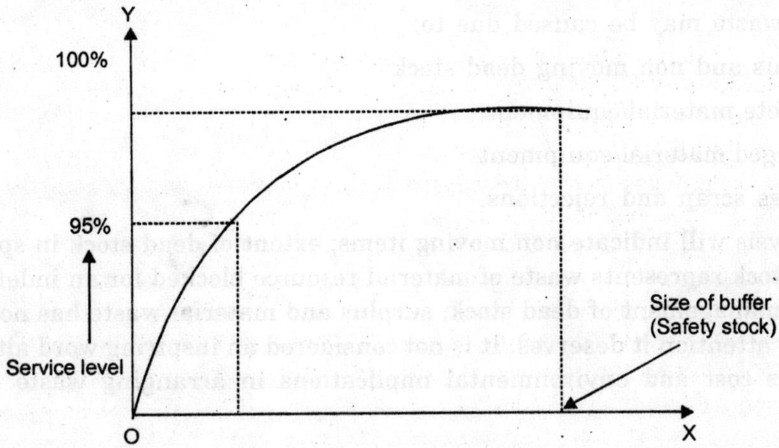

Fig. 2.23

Safety Stock When both Demand and Lead Time are Variable

$$S = \text{Safety stock} = K\sigma = \sqrt[K]{\bar{L}\sigma + \bar{D}\sigma L^2}$$

K = Constant corresponding to the acceptable risk of shortage in a lead time.

If the distance of lead time demand f(m) has a mean of $\bar{M}$ and standard deviation of σ then reorder point = $\bar{M} + S = \bar{M} + K\bar{\sigma}$. For given R one can compute the value of K and then the corresponding probability of shortage using normal table.

P(S) = Probability of shortage = 1 – P(s)

$$K = \frac{R - \bar{D}\bar{L}}{\sqrt{\bar{L}\sigma D^2 + \bar{D}^2\sigma L^2}}$$

K	p(s)	Service level
K = 1	p(s) = 15.9%	Service level 84.1%
1.2	11.5%	98.5%
1.3	10.0%	90.0%
2.0	0.3%	97.7%
2.5	0.6%	99.4%
3.0	0.1%	99.9%

Example: $\bar{L} = 3$ $\quad \sigma L = 1.45$ $\quad \bar{D} = 50$ $\quad \sigma D = 37.5$

$$\sigma = \sqrt{\bar{L}\sigma D^2 + \bar{D}\sigma L^2} = 73.7 \qquad R = 300$$

$$K = \frac{300 - 150}{73.7} = 2.04$$

P(S) = 2.1% stock out probability service level 97.9%

Waste Management

Material waste may be caused due to:

1. Surplus and non moving dead stock
2. Obsolete material/equipment
3. Damaged material/equipment
4. Process scrap and rejections.

FSN analysis will indicate non moving items; extent of dead stock in spares may be more. A dead stock represents waste of material resource blocked for an indefinite period. Unfortunately management of dead stock, surplus and material waste has not been given the managerial attention it deserves. It is not considered an inspiring word although there are tremendous cost and environmental implications in arranging waste of resources effectively.

Definition of Waste

Any unnecessary input and undesirable output form on the basis of resource wasted.

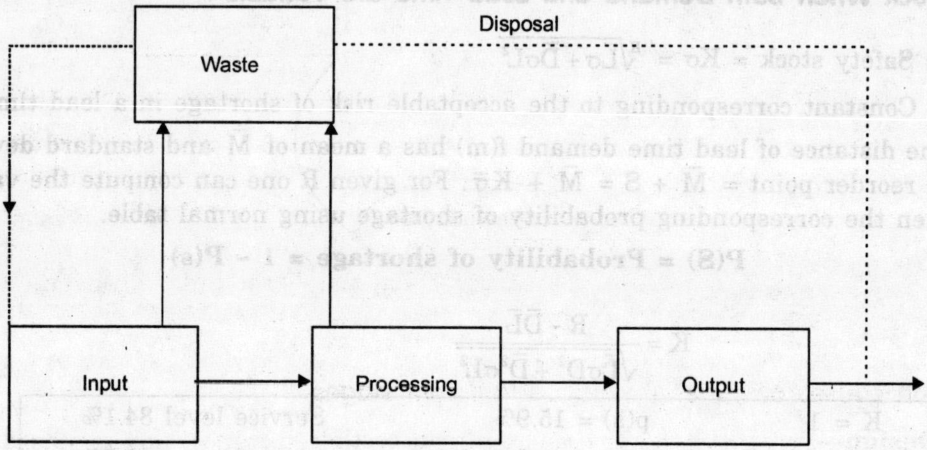

Fig. 2.24

Energy saving available through metal recycling and industry recycling targets.

Aluminium	Level of scrap recycling	Energy required to produce	Energy required
Copper	1,44,6000	Ton of metal from primary ore	
Iron/steel		51,379	
Lead			
Zinc			

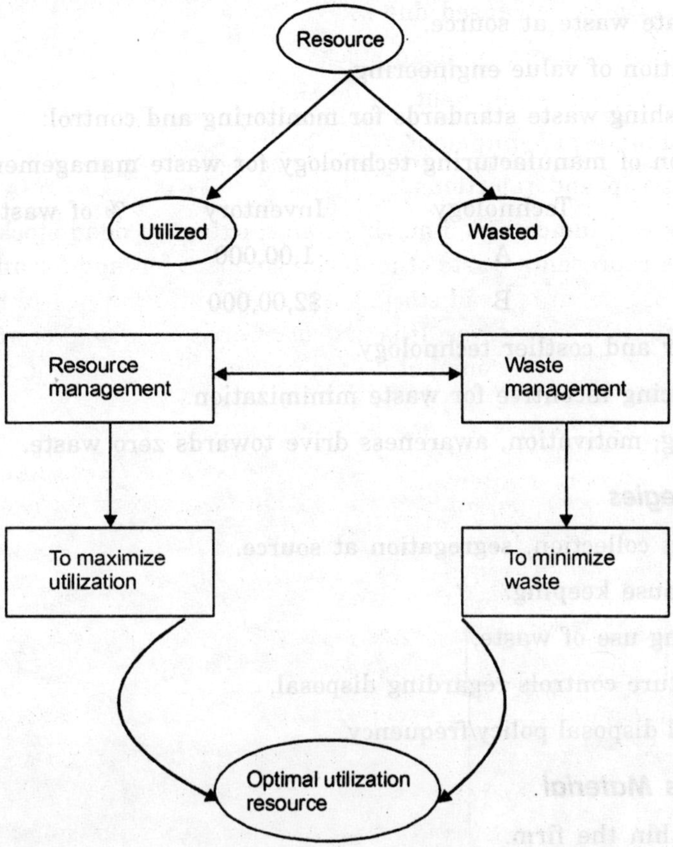

Fig. 2.25 Waste management and resource management

Identification causes of material waste at different stages

1. **Design**—Prescribed more than required, costlier material, non standard size. Tolerance can lead to waste of moving material.
2. **Purchase**—Overbuying, buying from wrong source, buying poor quality material may lead to waste of material resources.
3. **Storage**—Due to poor storage, material handling methods, material losses, damage, pilferage, evaporation during storage etc.
4. **Production**—Process scrap (Technology plays a role in waste generation), rejections, residues etc. By intelligent planning, effective production control and workmanship it can be reduced.
5. **Packaging/handling**—Material waste can get generated due to damage during transit, handling, due to poor packing.

Effective Waste Management

Best way to manage waste is not to generate it and get most out of whatever waste gets generated despite preventive steps through recycling.

Preventive Strategies

a. Eliminate waste at source.

b. Application of value engineering.

c. Establishing waste standards for monitoring and control:

Selection of manufacturing technology for waste management.

Illustration	Technology	Inventory	% of waste generation
	A	1,00,000	5%
	B	$2,00,000	2%

Cheaper and costlier technology.

d. Introducing incentive for waste minimization.

e. Training, motivation, awareness drive towards zero waste.

Corrective Strategies

1. Efficient collection, segregation at source.
2. Good house keeping.
3. Recycling use of waste.
4. Legislature controls regarding disposal.
5. Optimal disposal policy/frequency.

Disposal Surplus Material

1. Use within the firm.
2. Return to supplier.
3. Direct sales to another firm.
4. Sale to employee.
5. Sale to dealer/broker.
6. Donation.
7. Any other combination:

   a. Monitoring of waste.

   b. waste standard.

   c. Financial incentive for waste reduction.

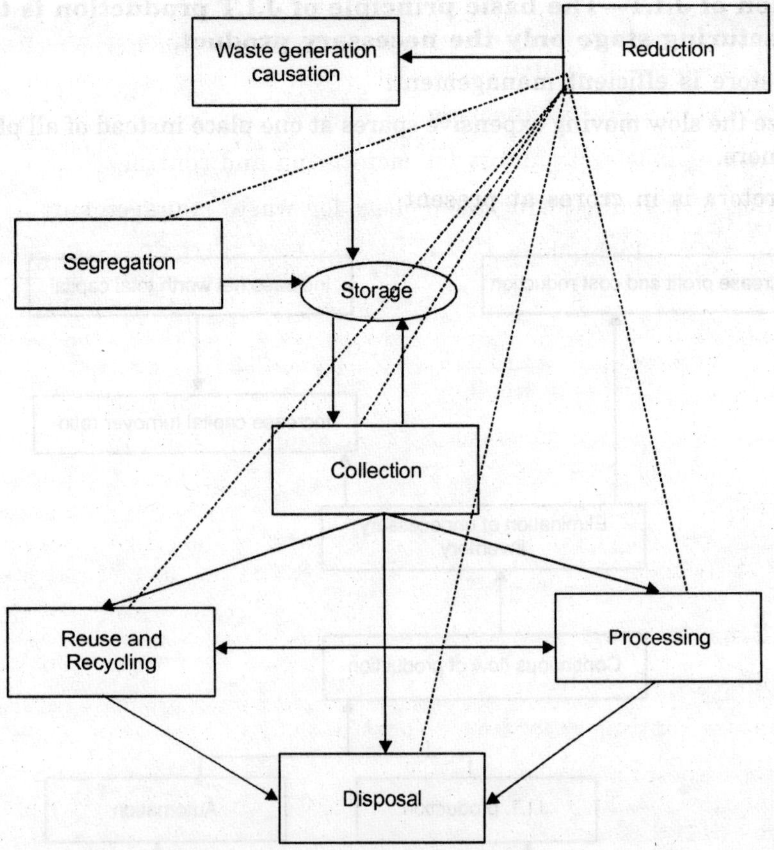

Fig. 2.26 Functional elements of waste management

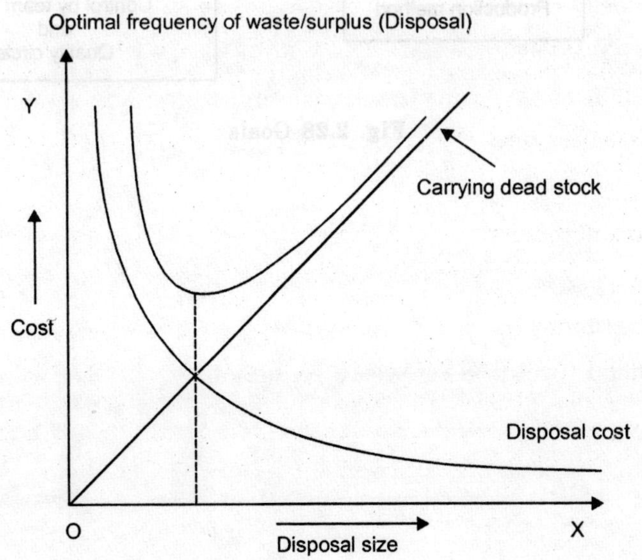

Fig. 2.27 Flow diagram of waste disposal system

Definition of J.I.T—The basic principle of J.I.T production is to produce at each manufacturing stage only the necessary product.

Central store is efficient management.

Centralize the slow moving expensive spares at one place instead of all places otherwise cost will be more.

Cost of rotors is in crores at present.

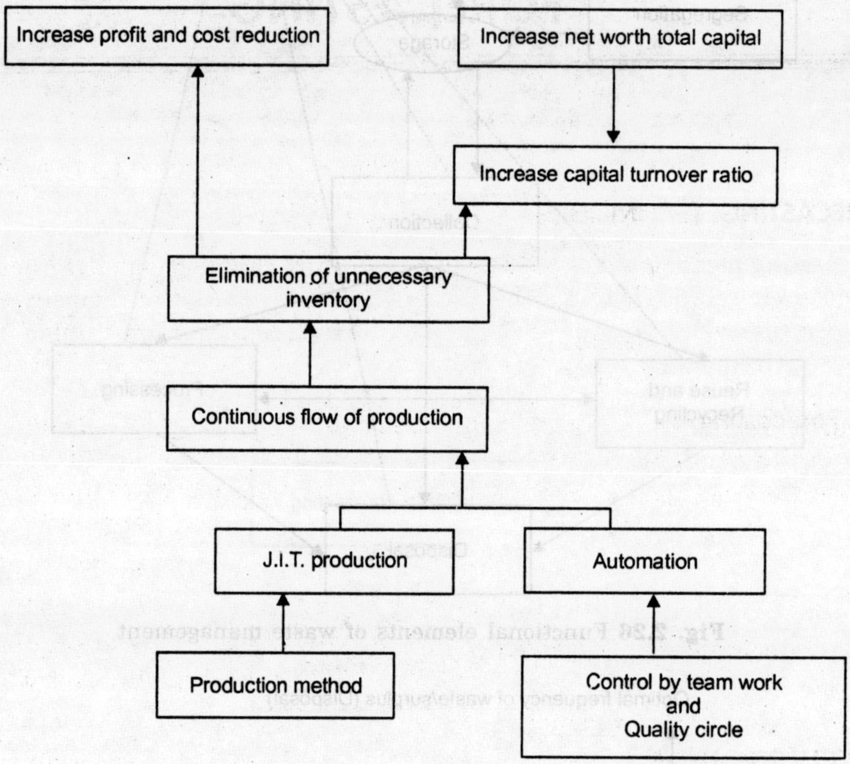

Fig. 2.28 Goals

3

CHAPTER

FORECASTING

3.1 FORECASTING TECHNIQUES

Forecasting means prediction. The plans of future cannot be made without forecasting events and their relationship. In the words of Philip Kotlers the company sales forecast is the expected level of company sales based on chosen marketing plan and assumed marketing environment.

Types of Forecasting

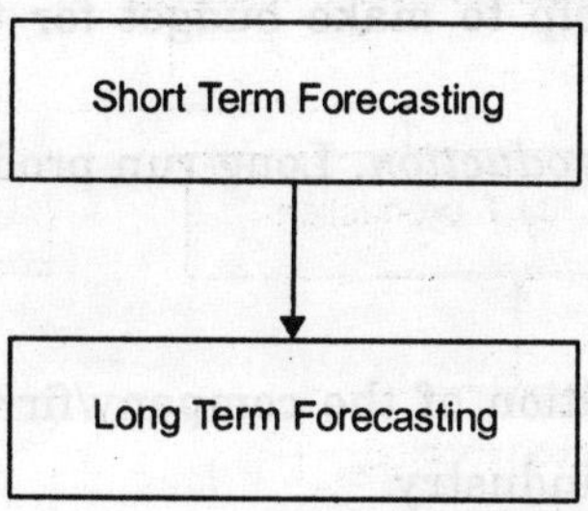

Short Term Forecasting

The forecasting which covers a short period like six months /one year is generally called as short term forecasting. Forecasting is done only when the demand fluctuates from one month to another.

Long-Term Forecasting

Forecasting done for five years or ten years comes under this category. Planning commission plans only for five years. As beyond ten years the future is assumed to be uncertain but wherever the initial cost of plant and machinery becomes more the forecasting is done for longer period as more amount is invested.

Objectives of Short-Term Forecasting

1. The suitable production policy plans can be prepared so that the problem of over-production or under-production may not arise.
2. Regular raw material requirement can be planned.

3. Machines can be fully utilized to recover the cost.
4. Regular availability of manpower can be assured so that there will not be loss of production. As sometimes it happens that due to shortage of manpower the machine becomes idle and work suffers. This affects mostly at the time of meeting the emergency demand.
5. Price of the commodity can be formulated as it always happens that there is inflation in the market. This forecasting helps the top management to plan for the future to avoid unnecessary losses during production.
6. Sales target can be achieved by having a proper forecasting. And if the forecasting of demand is not known every thing will go waste. For example, in functions of management if the planning is not done properly, the controlling makes no effect at all.

Objectives of Long-Term Forecasting

1. *Deciding the plant and machinery capacity*. As the sales forecasting can be made according to the plant capacity available in the organization with respect to the demand.
2. *Manpower planning*. Manpower planning for the long term requirement can be made.
3. *Budgetary control over expenditure*. As while making budget the information related to sales can help to make budget for the organization for income and expenditure.
4. *Planning of long run production*. Long run production planning also depends on sales forecasting.

Factors Affecting Forecasting

1. General business condition of the company/firm.
2. Conditions within the industry.
3. Govt rules and regulations and policies.
4. Price level and trend effects.
5. Substitution of latest technology.
6. Research and development.

Techniques of Forecasting

1. Executive Opinion Method.
2. Survey of Experts Opinion Method.
3. Sales Force Composite Method.
4. Survey of Buyers Intention Method.
5. Market Share Method.
6. Analytical and Statistical Method:
   (*i*) Sales trends analysis.
   (*ii*) Method of moving average.

(*iii*) Exponential smoothing.

(*iv*) Time series analysis.

(*v*) Regression analysis.

The forecasting can be done only by knowing the purpose of forecast and time period for which the forecasting is to be done, the benefits which the company will get after the forecast, the availability of time for forecasting.

Executive Opinion Method. This method is totally based on the experts' judgment. In this method the opinion of different executives of different fields are taken, like Marketing, Sales, Production, Finance. After brainstorming the experts give their views or opinion for the future forecast. For reliable forecast it is necessary that the experienced and persons with sound knowledge related to the forecast must be involved in forecasting.

3.2 MAKE OR BUY DECISION

Purchasing function is responsible for investigating all potential suppliers. Among them can be considered the buyer own firm—making parts or components within rather than buying it from an outside source of supply. This leads to a group of decisions known as MAKE/BUY DECISIONS.

These are important decisions as the optimal mix of make-buy will determine the key functional areas.

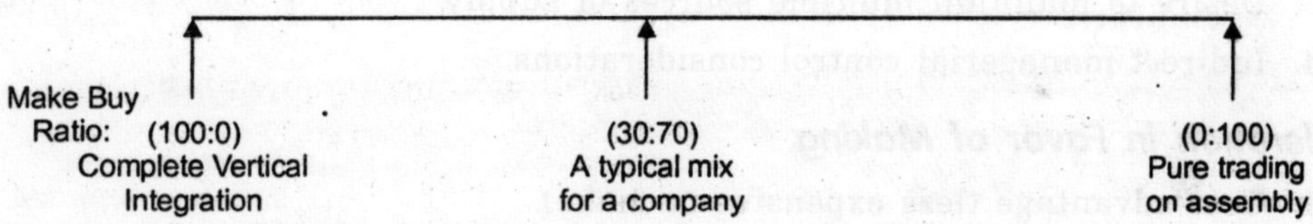

Fig. 3.1

Origination of Decision Problems

1. New products being planned.
2. Unsatisfactory vendor performances.
3. Value analysis—PPA.
4. Change in business demand.

Nature of Decision

It is assumed that capability already exists. Very minor capital investment is required in jigs, fixtures and tools without major capital investment in equipment.

Multiple Factors Relevant to Decision Making

1. Tangible (economic).
2. Intangible factors.
3. Availability of capacity.
4. Policy issue.

Cost concepts Needed in Such Decisions

We should employ incremental cost concept rather than conventional cost accounting data. Correct and accurate cost data should be developed otherwise it could lead to enormous decisions—buying parts which can be advantageously made within or vice versa.

Cost Consideration in Making

1. Delivered cost of raw materials.
2. Direct labor cost.
3. Incremental factory overhead.
4. Incremental managerial overhead.
5. Incremental purchasing cost.
6. Inventory carrying cost.
7. Incremental cost of capital investments.
8. Supplier research and specialized know-how.
9. Cost advantage (less expensive to buy).
10. Small volume requirement.
11. Limited production facilities—No spare capacity.
12. Policy to maintain stable workforce in retaining sales.
13. Desire to maintain multiple sources of supply.
14. Indirect managerial control considerations.

Consideration in Favor of Making

1. Cost advantage (less expensive to make).
2. Policy to integrate plant operations.
3. Productive use of excess plant capacity.
4. Need to exercise direct control on production or quality.
5. Design secrecy is required.
6. Unreliable suppliers.
7. Policy to maintain stable workforce in periods of declining sales.

Cost Relevant to Buying

1. Purchase prices.
2. Transportations.
3. Receiving and inspection.

Dynamic and Multi-Criteria Nature of Make/Buy Decisions

Dynamic and complex nature of business environment does not permit use of rigid formula—only cost advantage or rule of thumbs. Decisions are multiple criteria in nature and there should be a policy to review periodically the existing Make: Buy mix at higher management level rather than leaving it to operating personnel. There should be automatic review and proper records be maintained.

Use of decision matrix approach to Make/Buy decision:

Example

Demand for a certain type of costing is 600 per year. It can be die cast at factory at a cost of 46.31$. An outside supplier is willing to give it for 42.36$ per unit. Factory has spare capacity available to make it. Three factors considered relevant to decision making have following weightage:

Price 0.8; delivery schedule 0.3; capacity utilization 0.2

Alternative Make: Buy%	*Price advantage (0.5)*	*Delivery schedule (0.3)*	*Capacity utilization (0.2)*	*Total score*
100:00 (Make All)	50	90	90	70
75 : 25	60	80	85	71.5
50 : 50	60	69	70	69.5
25 : 75	77	60	55	67
00 : 100 (Buy All)	90	50	50	70

From this analysis 75:25 mix of make vs. buy will appear preferable although all alternatives are essentially comparable. We can develop some Heuristic rules like not to change the present decision unless cost advantage is more than 10% to avoid sensitive to cost alone.

Quality Assurance of Incoming Materials

Bitterness of poor quality lingers on after the sweetness of low price. Thus quality assurance plays a vital role in materials management. Quality must be built into the product rather than only inspected.

3.3 ACCEPTANCE SAMPLING

There are various techniques available to test samples. The major tools available in statistical quality control are:

1. Frequency Distribution
2. Sampling inspection or Acceptance sampling
3. Statistical quality control charts
4. Analysis of variance, tolerance and correlation

Quality of product can be checked by having 100% inspection of the product coming out of production machine or the purchased items for the raw materials. As in 100% inspection the time required will be more and the workers who are inspecting the items may be tired after some time as the same type of product/raw material is to be inspected for a longer time and there may be the chances of selecting the wrong samples or it may be possible that the wrong process is adopted to check. Due to the repetitive process and the fatigue there exists a possibility to overlook some defective parts and they may pass through the inspection process. Therefore, some system is to be adopted for sampling like picking up few samples from whole lot randomly and if the samples conform to the specifications desired then select it otherwise reject as the sample items are considered as the representative of the whole lot. This method of sampling is known as acceptance sampling.

Acceptance Sampling Classification

There are two ways to do acceptance sampling:

1. On the basis of attributes
2. On the basis of Variables

In acceptance sampling by variables the actual measurements of dimensions are taken or testing characteristics of materials. If the material meets the desired specifications, the lot is accepted otherwise rejected.

In acceptance sampling by attributes, no actual measurement is done and inspection is done by using different gauges, *i.e.*, Go or No Go gauges. If the product conforms to the desired specifications by using gauges the lot is accepted otherwise rejected. For example if spot on part is the criteria of inspection the product/parts to be rejected otherwise accepted. If cracks is the criteria of inspection/the products with creaks will be rejected and without cracks accepted the shape and size of the cracks shall not be measured and considered.

Advantages of Acceptance Sampling

This method can be easily learnt by the employees and they will be less tired. Employees can be trained easily. As the inspection time required is less the productivity can be improved. The maned is economical and easy to understand. The people involved in inception can be given training easily due to early inspection the scheduling and delivery time are improved.

Limitations of Acceptance Sampling

It does not give 100% assurance that the specification is correct, Receiving right sample depends on process of sampling randomness.

Producer's and Consumer's Risk

The result of the samples can only give the idea of acceptance/rejection of the product. There is always a chance that the sample may not be the true representative of the batches or lot from which it is drawn.

Producer's Risk

There is the probability of picking up the right sample and rejecting the same, so this type of probability of rejection of a good lot which otherwise would have been accepted is known as producers risk.

Consumer's Risk

There is the probability of getting a bad sample accepting the same. This probability of a defective sample/lot being accepted which otherwise would have been rejected is known as consumer's risk.

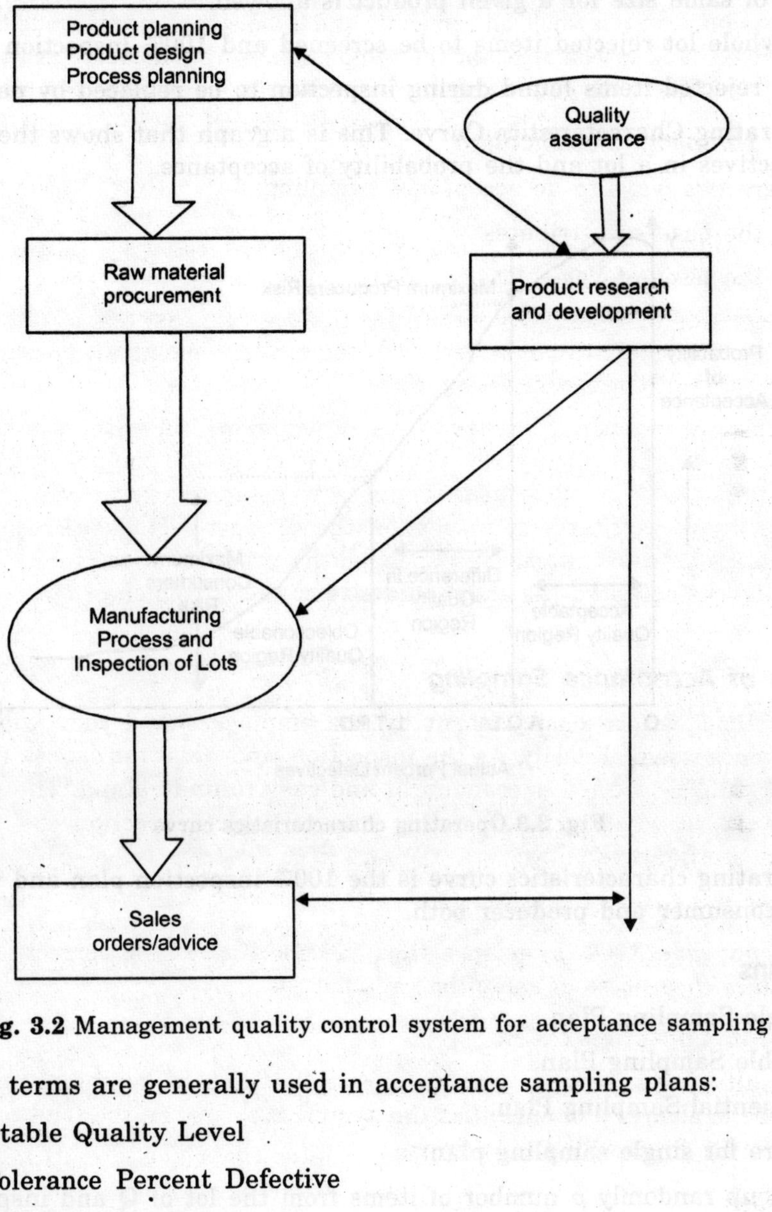

Fig. 3.2 Management quality control system for acceptance sampling

Following terms are generally used in acceptance sampling plans:

1. Acceptable Quality Level
2. Lot Tolerance Percent Defective
3. Average Outgoing Quality

A.Q.L. It represents the maximum proportion of defectives which the consumer accepts satisfactorty.

L.T.P.D. This gives the idea of good /bad lots.

A.O.Q. This shows that the average quality level or percentage defectives actually going to consumer will not exceed up to a certain limit. The A.O.Q can be defined as the ratio of actual defectives in the lot after inspection and total number of goods in the lot. Assumptions for the sampling plan can be taken as:

1. Lot of same size for a given product is allowed.
2. In whole lot rejected items to be screened and 100% inspection to be done.
3. The rejected items found during inspection to be replaced by new one.
4. Operating Characteristics Curve. This is a graph that shows the percentage of defectives in a lot and the probability of acceptance.

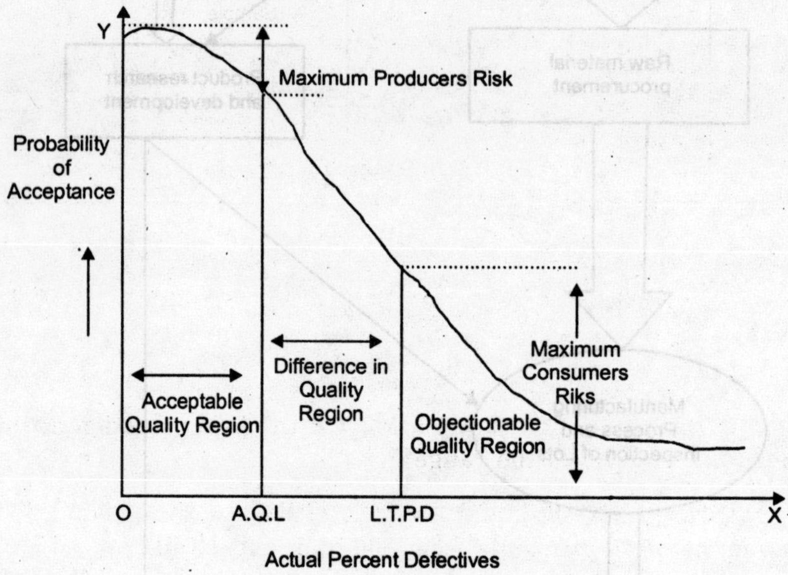

Fig. 3.3 Operating characteristics curve

The operating characteristics curve is the 100% inspection plan and will not create any risk for consumer and producer both.

Sampling Plans

1. Single Sampling Plan.
2. Double Sampling Plan.
3. Sequential Sampling Plan.

Procedure for single sampling plan:

1. Pick up randomly p number of items from the lot of Q and inspect them.
2. If the number of defectives found in the sample size are $\leq$ M, accept the lot
3. If the number of defectives in sample of p number of items > M, inspect the remaining (Q – p) items.
4. Replace or correct all the defective products found.

A sample containing p number of products is inspected, if the number of defective is below M1, the lot is accepted; if it is above the second acceptance number M2 where M2 > M1 the lot is rejected. If the number of defectives falls between M1 and M2 the result is inconclusive and a second sample is drawn.

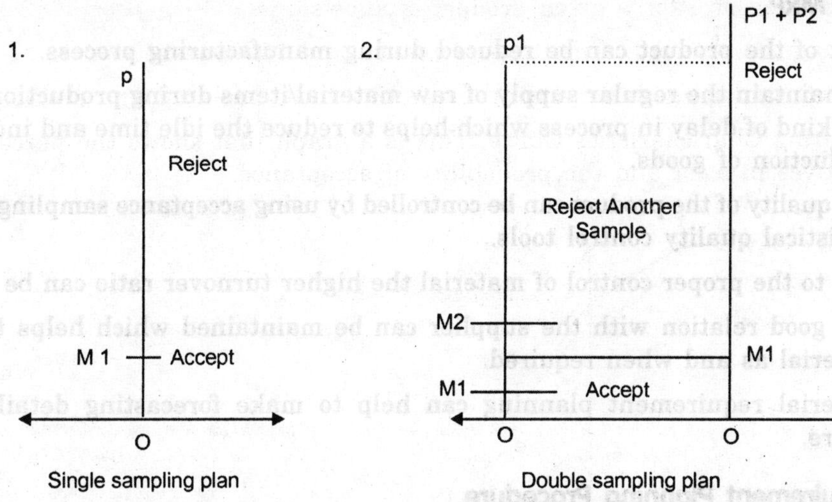

Fig. 3.4

Example

Let Q = 800, M1 = 2, P1 = 40, P2 = 60, M2 = 4 the interpretation of this data can be given as under. (M1 and M2 is the range)

1. The lot consists of 800 products.
2. Take a sample of 40 randomly from 800 and inspect all.
3. If the number of defectives are 2 accept the lot of 800 without further inspection.
4. If the number of defectives in 40 is more than 4 reject the whole lot of 800.
5. If the number of defectives in 40 is more than 2 but = 4 then take the second sample of 60 products from the remainder of Q *i.e.* from (800 – 40) and inspect these 60.

3.4 MATERIALS REQUIREMENT PLANNING

MRP stands for material requirement planning. It gives the clear picture of the requirement of raw material required in different phases of production and on the basis of this the plan for production schedule can be prepared. For any manufacturing process the inputs are required and the inputs like land and building, men, machine, raw material, electricity, water, pre-operative expenses, escalation and contingencies are used as the input, and in all these inputs the materials management plays a very important role and if the material requirement planning is done properly it can control the unnecessary cost spent on keeping raw material as the inventory. The material requirement planning helps to make the master production schedule. According to American Production and Control Society MRP constitutes a set of techniques that use bill of material, inventory data, and the master production schedule to calculate requirement for materials. This helps to make plan for reschedule orders adjustment as per the change in the need or requirement.

Objectives of MRP

1. Cost of the product can be reduced during manufacturing process.
2. To maintain the regular supply of raw material/items during production to avoid any kind of delay in process which helps to reduce the idle time and increase the production of goods.
3. The quality of the product can be controlled by using acceptance sampling methods/ statistical quality control tools.
4. Due to the proper control of material the higher turnover ratio can be obtained.
5. The good relation with the supplier can be maintained which helps to get the material as and when required.
6. Material requirement planning can help to make forecasting details for the future.

Material Requirement Planning Procedure

1. During planning for material the lead time must be taken in to consideration as the lead time means the procurement time, *i.e.*, the time taken for placing the order and receipt of material.
2. The environmental effect of the area where the industry is located can affect the demand due to seasonal variation fluctuation.
3. When planning is done for the shorter period the reliable effect may be obtained by the company.
4. Computer aided development programs to be used wherever possible to save time.

Concepts Used in Material Planning

1. Lead Time is the time required from the initial stage to the finished stage. The total time to be taken for the purchase and the items to be manufactured must be known and can be categorized into two types of lead time.

   (*a*) Manufacturing Lead Time

   (*b*) Ordering Lead Time

Manufacturing lead time is the time required for processing of product through the sequence of machinery available in factory or work stations. The lead time includes the time of processing, idle time, waiting time, loading/unloading time, movement of worker time working on various machines, tool set up time etc.

Ordering Lead Time

It is the time required for the purchase of raw material during the process of purchase and receipt of material at works for production. In this case the purchase department becomes fully dependent on the supplier. Due to this reason the ABC analysis and VED analysis is done.

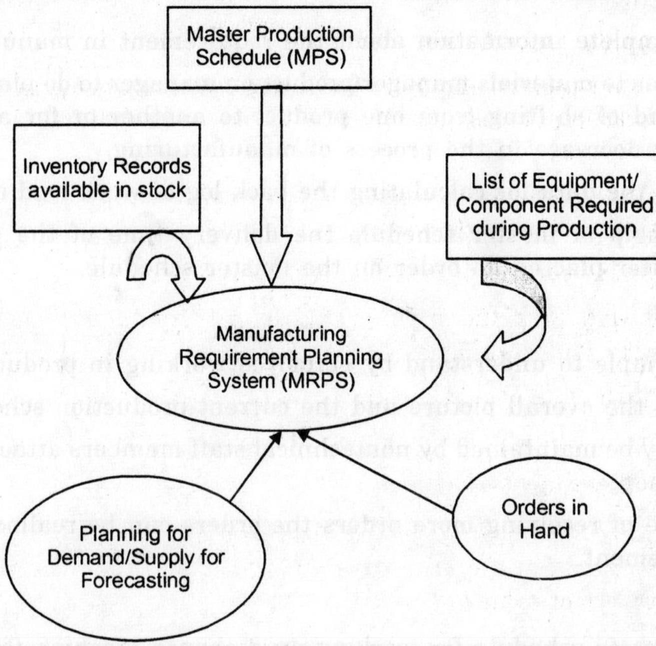

Fig. 3.5 Manufacturing requirement planning input system

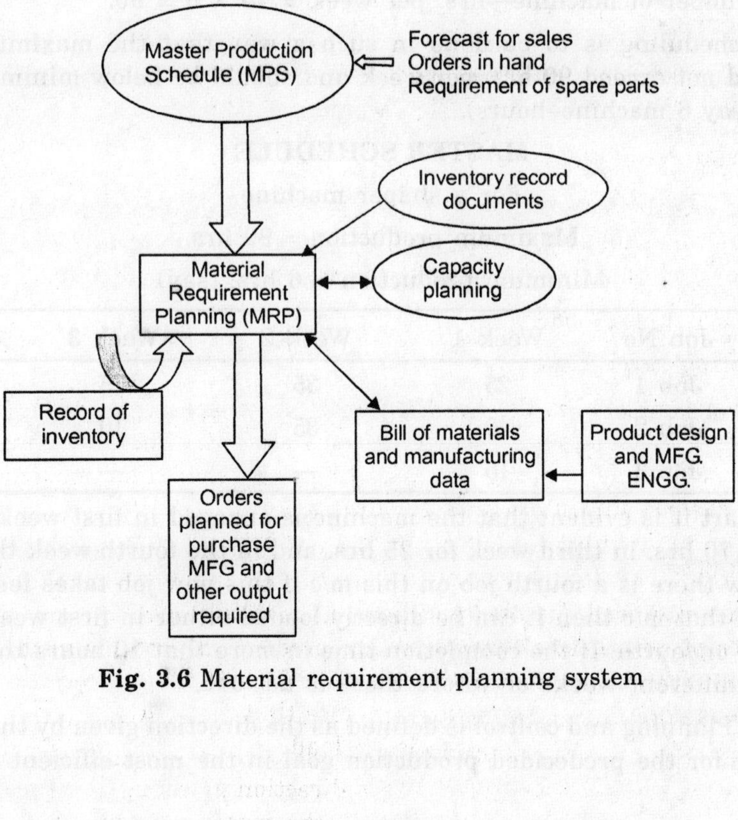

Fig. 3.6 Material requirement planning system

3.5 OBJECTIVES OF MASTER SCHEDULE

1. It gives complete information about the requirement in manufacturing.
2. It gives ideas to materials manager/production manager to do planning in advance for any kind of shifting from one product to another or for a possible overall increase or decrease in the process of manufacturing.
3. It provides the data for calculating the back log of work load on each machine.
4. With the help of master schedule the delivery time of the customer can be finalized after placing an order on the master schedule.

Advantages

1. It's vary simple to understand by employee working in production hall.
2. It provides the overall picture and the current-production schedule.
3. It can easily be maintained by nontechnical staff members attached to workshop/ machine shop.
4. At the time of receiving more orders the orders can be reallocated/adjusted as per requirement.

Example

Prepare the master schedule for working on a shaper machine for a month.

From the past data it is known that the machine works 15 hrs. a day.

So more number of machine—hrs. per week = 15 × 6 = 90.

Now the scheduling is to be done in such a way that the maximum number of m/c hours should not exceed 90 hrs. per week and should be below minimum number of machine—hrs. (say 6 machine–hours).

MASTER SCHEDULE

For a shaper machine

Maximum production = 90 hrs.

Minimum production = 6 hrs. (say)

S.No.	Job No	Week 1	Week 2	Week 3	Week 4
1	Job 1	25	35	15	—
2	Job 2	40	35	10	—
3	Job 3	15	—	—	—

For this chart it is evident that the machine is engaged in first week for 80 hrs, in second week for 70 hrs. in third week for 25 hrs. and in the fourth week there is no load on machine. Now there is a fourth job on this m/c if this new job takes less then 10 hrs. in processing on that m/c then it can be directly loaded either in first week or in second week or in third or fourth. If the completion time in more that 10 hours then the job has to be loaded in different weeks or where there is no load.

Production Planning and control is defined as the direction given by the firm towards the achievement for the predecided production goal in the most efficient way.

4
CHAPTER
PURCHASE ORGANIZATION

4.1 PURCHASE ROLE IN QUALITY ASSURANCE

It is the responsibility of the purchase department to ensure that suppliers (vendors) possess the ability, the motivation and adequate information to produce and supply materials and components in a cost effective manner.

Quality assurance calls for preventive and corrective strategies. Four factors determine long run quality level of a firm's purchased materials:

1. Creation of complete and appropriate specifications. These should be unambiguously communicated to the supplier to prevent miss-interpretation and avoid quality problems to crop up later on.
2. Selection of suppliers (Source selection having technical, production capabilities to do an adequate quality/cost job. Get best value for money paid.)
3. Development of realistic understanding with the vendor and creating positive motivation. (vendor relationship)
4. Excessive control through performance appraisal of supplier, through inspection (vender rating).

Source Selection, Source Development and Evaluation

A dependable supplier (source or vendor) is a major asset to the materials management function. Inventory can be substantially reduced by having an enlightened source of supply to facilitate Just-in-Time planning.

Attributes of a Good Vendor

1. *Quality.* Process capability, Quality consciousness and Quality culture.
2. *Quantity.* Financially sound, honest/fair in dealing with the customer.
3. *Price.* Reasonable price, unity of interests.
4. *Delivery schedule.* Adequate production capacity, capacity to keep process stocks.

Other intangible attributes such as dependability (reliability), convenience, availability, after sales service, sales assistance, etc., may be check listed.

Vendor Analysis

Detailed multi-criteria evaluation into supplier's capability (financial, technical, process capability, quality, after sales service, transport facilities, in plant testing facilities, other clients, price, location, lead-times, dependability, reputation, etc.) in order to select the best source of supply.

Material Specification

1. Design.
2. Production.
3. Commissioning considerations:
   - (*i*) Study quality requirements and study the reasonable use to costs.
   - (*ii*) Can desired quality be built by present supplier?
   - (*iii*) Write specifications to permit competition among potential suppliers.
   - (*iv*) Quality specifications should be unambiguously and completely stated in order to avoid problems later on.

Selection of Suppliers (Source selection)

An enlightened supplier is the major assets to an effective materials management function. Best control is to pick up a right source. Some preliminary checks are:

1. *Product Testing.* Get the product quality tested in-house or in test houses before interacting.
2. *Proposal analysis.* Thoroughly examine the tender response regarding supplier's interaction, supply quality, any ambiguity in response.
3. *Capability surveys.* Process capability analysis checks 6*x* range with quality specifications, production/financial capabilities, reputation and reliability. Whether he is quality conscious, quality assurance program like Operation Research, SQC etc.

Source Development

Source development is the process of developing, activating new sources of supplies of materials in order to improve the supply sources. It requires continued support, interaction to develop a source and may take years.

Top management must give high priority to source development to improve supply environment. The need for source development may arise due to the following reasons:

1. For new items.
2. Poor performance of an existing supplier upon vendor rating or PPA/VA.
3. Technical constraints on existing supplier.
4. Management policy to maintain multiple supply sources to encourage competition.
5. Govt policy to develop ancillary industries.

4.2 PURCHASE PRICE ANALYSIS (PPA)

In PPA an attempt is made to identify the gap between the price charged and fair price; larger the gap, more the need for source development as the present supplier is not the best one. Value analysis also reveals the need for source development.

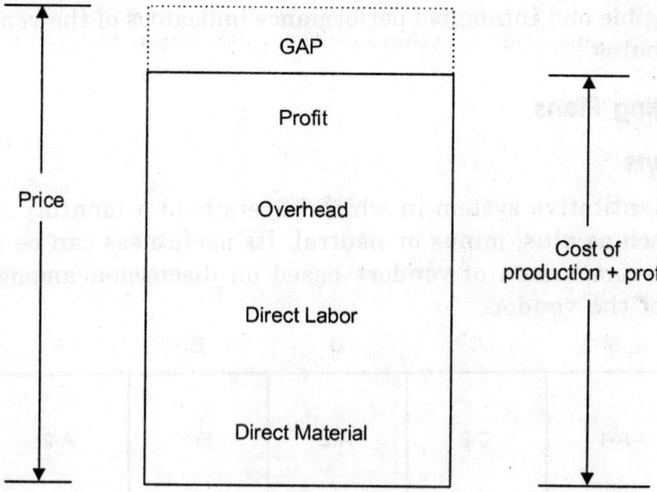

Fig. 4.1

Vendor Rating (VR)

Vendor rating is an objective, periodic and meaningful performance appraisal of an existing source of supply (vendor) which motivates good performance and discourages poor performance. The crucial thing is objectivity and the supplier confidence in the evaluation process. Hence vendor participation in evolving an evaluation scheme is an useful strategy. Vendor rating is not a tool for making decision on submitted lots. Vendor rating must be periodic to generate suppliers' performance records. This analysis should evaluate whether he is improving or going down in over-all performance indicators.

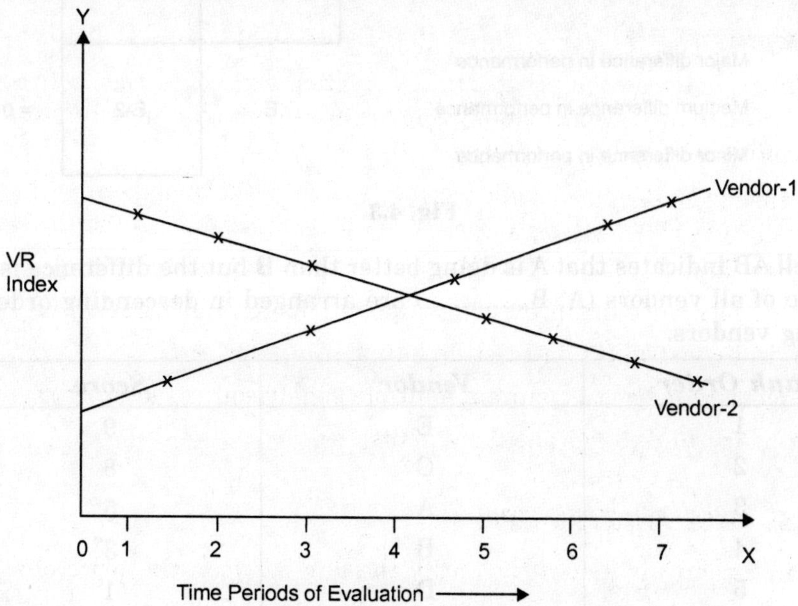

Fig. 4.2

Vendor rating must create a healthy feeling of fair competition among vendors. This could be done by instituting award for the best vendor performance during the year; by awarding further contracts to high performers etc. However, VR must be a composite index of various tangible and intangible performance indicators of the vendor in measurable terms on key attributes.

Various Vendor Rating Plans

Categorization Plans

This is non quantitative system in which buyers hold a monthly meeting to discuss vendors and rate each as plus, minus or neutral. Its usefulness can be possibly improved by having a paired–comparison of vendors based on discussion among management on various attributes of the vendor.

	B	C	D	E	F	
A	A-1	C-3	A-2	E-1	A-2	= 5
	B	C-2	B-2	E-1	B-1	= 3
		C	C-1	E-3	C-2	= 8
			D	E-2	D-1	= 1
				E	E-2	= 0

3 Major difference in performance

2 Medium difference in performance

1 Minor difference in performance

Fig. 4.3

A–1 in cell AB indicates that A is doing better than B but the difference is only minor. The total score of all vendors (A, B,............) are arranged in descending order to get the ranking among vendors.

Rank Order	*Vendor*	*Score*
1	E	9
2	C	8
3	A	5
4	B	3
5	D	1
6	F	0

Weighted-Point Plan

Each vendor is scored on various factors like quality, price, service etc. Factors are weighted and a composite VR index is obtained as follows:

(*i*) *Quality Rating*. R Q = (Q1 + x1. Q1 + Q3. x2/Q × 100)

where		
	Q =	Quantity supplied
	Q1 =	Quantity accepted
	Q2 =	Quantity accepted with concessions
	Q3 =	Accepted with rectification
	Q4 =	Quantity rejected
		X*i* are weightage factors, x*i* = 1
(*ii*) *Price Rating.*	Rp =	PL/P × 100
	PL =	Lowest price quoted
	P =	Price agreed by supplier
(*iii*) *Delivery Rating.*	RD =	No. of orders received on time/ Total no. of orders placed × 100
(*iv*) *Quantity Rating.*	Rq =	Q/Qp × 100
	Q =	Qty. supplied within time
	Q *p* =	Qty promised

(*v*) *Service Rating* (R1). It is an intangible rating to be assigned based on factors such as:

S .No	*Service Factor*	*Max. Score.*
1.	Co-operativeness/help in emergencies	Q1
2.	Readiness to replace rejected materials	Q2
3.	Provide support document in time	Q3
4.	Promptness in reply	Q4
5.	Acceptance of terms without complains	Q5
		100

The composite vendor performance Rating (VPR),

VPR = *fi*. R*q* + *f*2Rp + *f*3Rp + *f*4R4 + *f*5. Rs

Where fi are weight factor of ith rating

Example

Weight	Factor		Measurement Formula
50%	Quality	=	100%-% of rejection
25%	Service	=	100%-7% for each failure.
25%	Price	=	Lowest price/Actual price

If a vendor had 5% rejects; 3 unsatisfactory split shipment; price \$ 100 compared to \$ 90 as the lowest price. VPR?

VPR = 50 (1 – 0.05) + 25 (1 – 0.07 × 3) + 25 (90/100) = 89.75%

Cost Ratio Plan

Opportunity cost of delayed supplies, poor quality, returning of rejected lots, freight charges etc.

Cost ratio are computed such as

(*i*) Quality cost ratio ⟶ Rejects relative quality related cost.

(*ii*) Delivery cost ratio ⟶ Rejects cost of placing and receiving cost.

(*iii*) Service cost ratio ⟶ Rejects technical, managerial and field service competence of the supplier.

These cost ratios are then used for adjusting the unit price quoted by the supplier.

Example

Quality cost ratio = 1.02; (+ 2% cost) Quoted price = $72.25

Delivery cost ratio = 1.02; (+ 2% cost)

Service cost ratio = 0.99; (– 1% cost)

Overall cost ratio = 2 + 2 – 1 = 3%

Adjusted price = 1.03 × 72.25 = $74.45

This system calls for efficient, computerized cost accounting system. It tends to be complex and hence not much in use.

4.3 OBTAINING RIGHT PRICE THROUGH EFFECTIVE PURCHASING

Purchasing function is responsible for spending more than half of total company finances and may be great risk to play towards cost reductions by reducing the direct visible costs of purchases.

By using right type of strategies and skills it should be possible to reduce material price by 15% for 10% profit margin. 50% purchase cost is equivalent to 75% increase in sales in terms of profitability. Increasing sales by 75% is very difficult if steady state conditions are achieved. Study shows that effective purchasing should return 300-500% of its own cost. 20-30% of corporate savings must come from purchases savings and cost reduction programmes.

Objective

Right quantity, right quality, right source, right time, right price.

Obtaining right price:

1. Published price list
2. Competitive bidding (closed/open)
3. Price negotiations
4. Price investigations (Purchase price)
5. Price tenders comparison
6. Price discounts—seasonal, quantity, cost.

When to Negotiate

Whenever competitive bidding is impractical.

Negotiation Process

SWOT analysis: Strength, Weakness, Opportunities and threats.

S, W refers to past, O, T, refers to potential future.

Seller's Strength

1. Seller's desire for a contract lesser his desire, greater his strength
2. Seller's certainty of getting a contract.
3. Time available/urgency of suppliers—emergency buying leads to selling's strength.

Buyer's Strength

1. The extent of competition
2. Cost analysis/PPA. If PPA can reveal huge profits it could be used to negotiate price reduction.
3. Thoroughness of preparation. Using A-B-C analysis for price negotiations, selectively identify crucial items on which to negotiate-select few.

Purchase Price Negotiation for Effective Materials Management

Bill negotiation is one of the most interesting as well as most important parts of professional purchasing function. Because the process is complex and costly it should be selectively used primarily for high usage value items.

Negotiations

Conferring, discussing or bargaining to reach agreement in business transactions with the following objectives:

1. To obtain a fair and reasonable price for the quality specified.
2. To get the supplier to perform the contract on time.
3. To exert some control over the manner the contract is performed.
4. To make supplier to provide maximum cooperation to buyers.
5. To develop sound and continuing vendor relationship.

When to Negotiate

Negotiation is effective when the competitive bidding is impractical.

Buyer's Role in Negotiation Process

1. Acting alone.
2. Leader of a team.

In case of team negotiation a careful planning, rehearsal is needed so that each investor carries on a pre-assigned task and does not speak out of turn.

Negotiation Process

Buyer must see in terms of total cost and total value and not unit price alone.

Strength/Weakness Analysis

SWOT Analysis/Pareto Analysis and gains theoretic analysis are helpful in the process of negotiation.

Seller's strength	*Buyer's strength*
1. Seller's desire for a contract	1. Extent of competition
2. Seller's certainty of getting a contract	2. Purchase Price Analysis
3. Time available for negotiations	3. Thorough preparation

Techniques of Negotiations

1. Organize issues.
2. Be sure of seller's authority to negotiate.
3. Negotiate on home grounds.
4. Keep the initiative.
5. Use questions effectively and use positive statements.
6. Be a good listener.
7. Be considerate to sellers.
8. Benefits are not divided equally.
9. Prolonged silence.
10. Offensive/defensive strategies etc.
11. Price analysis.

Objective of Good Purchasing

1. Procurement of the right material, in the right quantity, and of the right quality.
2. Receipt or delivery of this material at the right place and at the right time.
3. Purchase of the material from the right source and at the right price.

Purchasing Procedure

The complete purchase cycle consists of the following steps:

1. Receipt and analysis of the purchase requisition.
2. Selection of potential source of supply.
3. Issuance of request for quotation.
4. Receipt and analysis of quotations.
5. Selection of the right source.
6. Determination of the right source.
7. Issuance of the purchase order.
8. Follow up to ensure scheduled delivery.
9. Analysis of received reports'.
10. Analysis and approval of vendor's invoice for payment.

4.4 VALUE ANALYSIS

An activity that is closely related to both improvement programs and purchasing and that is being used extensively in industry and the Govt is value analysis. Value analysis is an objective study of every item of cost in every component part, subassembly, or price of equipment. This includes a study of the design, the material and the process in a continual search for other possible materials and new processes. Value analysis involves the evolution of an item's function and relates its effect on the end product. The purpose of it is to ensure that every element of cost contributes proportionately to the function of the item. Just as in work simplification approach, value analysis uses a questioning attitude and ask some key questions:

1. What is it?
2. What does it do?
3. What does it cost?
4. What is its worth?
5. What else will do the job?
6. How much will it cost?

It is obvious from the question that value analysis is connected with function, cost and value. It probably tends to put more emphasis on materials than the traditional method analysis or work simplification program. At the same time, it is an important ingredient of a total cost reduction program.

The objective of the value analysis is to get more value from an item in terms of function. This can and should be done whether the item is manufactured within the plant or purchased from outside. Outside purchases make it relatively easy to evaluate savings since there is often difference in quoted prices for the items, and the difference is a real savings to the company. The General Electrical company pioneered value analysis work, and we cite one or two of their experiences to illustrate what is meant by this process. One of their part was a push button that had been made as a screw machine part. Investigation among suppliers resulted in a push button that could be cold headed from aluminium wire. Cost of item dropped from nineteen cents to two cents. Another part was a steel J bolt with threads on the long end. The drawing simply said cut thread. A rolled thread specialist studied the part and suggested that the words cut thread be removed from the drawing thereby making it possible to roll the thread. This was done and the part could then be purchased at 1.5 cents as compared to 11.7 cents formerly. The company saved 80,000 dollars. In both of the cases cited the function of the part remained the same, and the new part could perform this function as well as the old. The difference was the tremendous savings in cost of purchase, hence value of the part increased enormously.

Factors Affecting Purchasing

1. Requisitioning authority.
2. Type of manufacture.
3. Sub contracting.
4. Standardization of the product.
5. Economic purchase lot.
6. Short and controlled markets.
7. Cancellations.
8. Trade relations.

Requisitioning Authority

No purchases should be made without a properly signed purchase requisition. The first and most important step in the control of materials is the control of the authority to sign purchase requisition. Authority to sign purchase requisitions should be limited to as few individual as possible.

Type of Manufacture

The type of manufacture influences the purchasing activity. Continuous manufacturing industries such as those that produce radios and automobiles normally operate extensive assembly lines. Material is scheduled to these lines with a minimum of stock inventory and the majority of the control of material becomes the responsibility of the purchasing group.

Evaluation of Purchasing

As an overall activity it is difficult to make a valid evaluation of the purchasing activity. General measures such as the ratio of the cost of purchasing to the value of material purchased, or to the value of sales, may provide a useful index within a given organization. It is easier to set up measures related to the more specific objectives of the purchasing group: is the right material of the right quality and in right quantity being procured from the right source at the right price and delivered at the right place and at the right time? Continuous rating of the accomplishment of these objectives will indicate the success of the function if not the total efficiency. So far as these objectives might be accomplished at excessive cost by the purchasing organization it might be well to consider the ratio of purchasing costs to the profits of the concern—but again so many factors affect these profits that a valid measurement is highly doubtful.

4.5 ORGANIZATION OF PURCHASING FUNCTION

The importance of purchasing function varies with the nature and size of industry. In small factories this function is performed by the works manager but in larger manufacturing concerns, where large quantities of materials are consumed, the buying function is given to a separate department under a highly competent executive designated as chief buyer. The cost of direct and indirect material form a part of the prime cost of the product. Careful buying helps in reducing the cost of materials and there by increasing the profits. Hence purchasing is one of the delicate activities and the persons employed should be sincere, honest and intelligent.

4.6 FUNCTIONS OF PURCHASING DEPARTMENT

1. To purchase materials on properly authorized requisitions..
2. The place orders for the requisitioned goods with right suppliers.
3. To obtain right type and quality of goods at cheapest price.
4. To purchase right qualities in right time.
5. To see that deliveries of all goods are received with in time.
6. To check and see that goods received are in accordance with the orders placed in respect of quality, quantity and specifications.

7. To study the market conditions and enter into a rate contract with the large suppliers to ensure availability of materials all the time.
8. To study the various sources of supply and decide upon the most convenient as well as alternate suppliers.
9. To keep the list of available and reliable suppliers.
10. To prepare specification to obtain quotations and compare these quotations and placing orders.
11. To look that suppliers payments are made promptly so that public relations are maintained.
12. To purchase directly all small items which do not require quotations.

4.7 METHODS OF PURCHASING

(*a*) Purchasing strictly by requirement
(*b*) Purchasing for a specified period
(*c*) Market purchasing
(*d*) Contract purchasing
(*e*) Central purchase organization
(*f*) Through Directorate General of Supplies and Disposals.

Purchase Procedure

The following purchase procedures are adopted according to the situations.

1. Local purchase system
2. Single tender system
3. Closed tender system
4. Open tender system

All these are described in bring below:

1. *Local Purchase System.* In purchasing small items or in case of emergency the material is purchased locally by cash payment or without obtaining quotations. The rates may be confirmed orally or by phone or by some other means and order is placed on the spot. This system contains no clerical work and time, quality and availability are the prime consideration than price. This system is adopted mostly in hand to mouth purchasing.

2. *Single Tender System.* When the quality is of extreme importance only a reliable firm will be asked to supply and rates are fixed by material acceptance. In this when he sales are on decline, the customer will be very happy to receive orders for the material, he can supply can the firms will also try to increase the turnover by placing orders on the customer slightly higher rates.

3. *Closed Tender System.* When material is required, firms which are registered will be invited to tender their rates is sealed envelope, the tender is opened and who so ever quotes the lowest rate bid goes in his favour. As in this system only the registered firms are invited this system is called united system.

4. *Open Tender System.* This is also called unlimited tender system, since the quantities

to he purchased involves large amount. A tender notice in trade journals and news paper is published by giving the detailed specification of the item required and period and place of delivery and other terms and conditions are published in news paper. After receiving all the tenders in sealed cover the tender is opened in the presence of all the firms representative on the particular date at the presented place and time. The various firms comparative is prepared and who so ever quotes the lowest rates the order goes in his favour. In case the supplier refuse to supply on the prescribed lowest rate the order is given to the next firm who so ever has quoted the next lowest rate and the earnest money or security money deposit of firm is forefeited.

Centralized and Decentralized Purchasing Function

Centralized purchase. In this kind of purchase all the purchase is done at the Head office of the organization and the supply effects through Head office to the branch office. This normally happens in Govt. Department.

Decentralized purchase. In this the power of purchase is decentralized to branch office to avoid delay in receiving raw material well on time. This happen in multinational companies. The manufacturing company which is running several plants at different locations and manufacture different items and have different type of material requirement there the system of decentralized purchase is used. At each plant the financial power is delegated to purchase items as per there requirement.

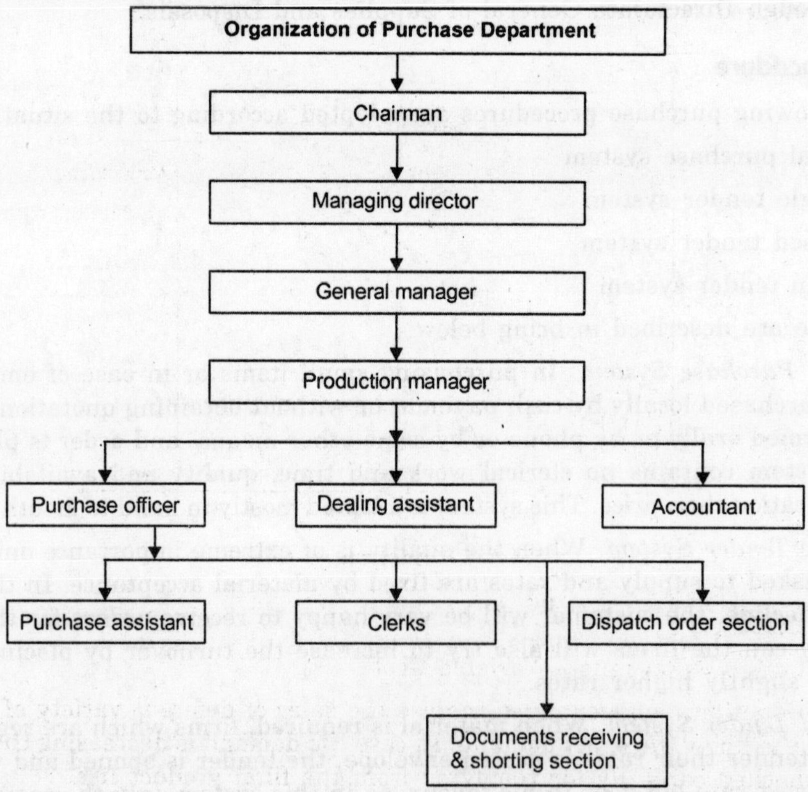

Fig. 4.4

4.8 VARIETY REDUCTION

By reducing the varity of products during production process the cost, mfg time, scheduled delivery time can be reduced. For this purpose cellular manufacturing system is used. In this system the small group of machines usually dissimilar injunction are grouped into a cell, then a cell should ideally be responsible for the complete processing of a group of parts called a part family. Cell formation is a complex problem is the design of CMS. Cell formation consists of identifying part families (PFS) and machine groups (MG)s. By reducing the variety the work on lathe m/c or any other m/c the time required to use jig and fixture every time can be reduced for changing job every time which will increase production.

It always happens that the designers makes the typical design or complicated design due to which it becomes difficult to manufacturer to give more time in production and due to variety of designs the process takes time. The standardization helps to reduce variety of parts to manufacture. Marketing manager always wants to have the variety of items to be sold in market to meet the different demands in market. To shortout the problem of sales the standardization is done by reducing variety of parts.

4.9 TECHNIQUES OF VARIETY REDUCTION

1. Analysis of Sales
2. Annual Consumption Analysis
3. Preferred Numbers

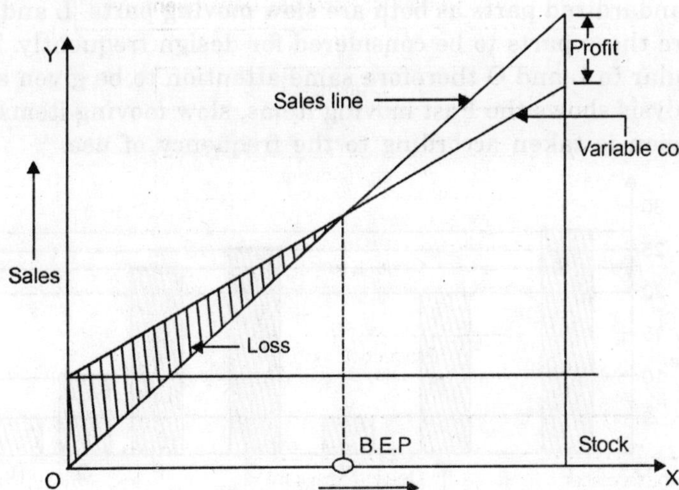

Fig. 4.5 Analysis of sales

Analysis of Sales

Contribution = Revenue – Variable Cost

The production manager must analyse the sales of deferent variety of products and keep arecard to know the exact demand. In case the demand is decreasing the contribution should be checked carefully for removing from the final product list.

Annual Consumption Analysis

This analysis gives the exact figure of consumption of raw material during production and the row material which is not used frequently. The systematic annual consumption analysis will give the idea to which item to be produced and which item to be deleted from the list by the material menaper/production manoper. As at present cellular manufacture system are used in which small group % m/s are kept and identification of past families are done to reduced production cost.

Example

Standardized parts v/s frequency of using parts mfd.

Table 4.1

Standardized parts	Frequency of use
L	25
M	20
N	4
O	21
P	22
Q	10
R	4

The above table shows that part R and N is used rarely therefore these parts to be deleted from the standardized parts as both are slow moving parts. L and O are used most of the time therefore these parts to be considered for design frequently. The parts M and P are also used similar to L and O therefore same attention to be given as given to L and O. As F – S – N analysis shows the Fast moving items, slow moving items and non moving items and the decision is taken according to the frequency of use.

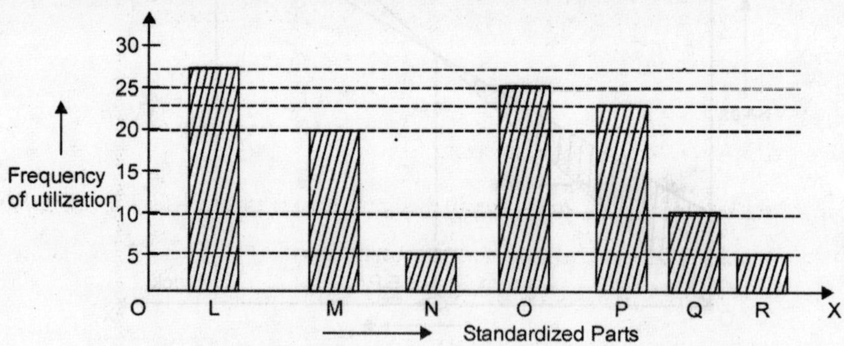

Fig. 4.6 Standardized parts VS frequency of utilization

Preferred Numbers

According to the American Standards Association, preferred numbers are a series of number selected to be used for standardization purposes in preference to other numbers. The problem of selecting preferred numbers was first tackled by the french engineer col. Charles Renard in 1870 and, therefore the series is sometimes referred to as the Renard series. Renard was an officer in the French Army and faced the problem of 425 different sizes of cables when are in use in his unit. He recognized that the process of standardization consisted of two problems to define the number of terms in the series and to determine

5

CHAPTER

STORES MANAGEMENT

5.1 STORES MANAGEMENT

The scope of the stores function is to look after effectively and efficiently the physical custody of materials after their acquisition until these are issued for production use.

Functions

1. Receiving and inspection.
2. Storage.
3. Retrieval and issue.
4. Stock accounting.
5. Physical stock verification.

Performance Criteria for the Effectiveness of Stores Management

1. Stores efficiency index—pending indents, retrieval time.
2. Handling loss index.
3. Storage loss index.
4. Space utilization and housekeeping.

Decision Associated with Design and Operation of Storage and Retrieval Systems

1. Storage location—Centralized vs. Decentralized.
2. Storage layout planning—Objectives and guidelines.
3. Storage methods—bins, rack, platforms, buckets, shelves etc.
4. Storage systems—open, closed, dedicated random access.
5. Material identification code and stores address system.
6. Issue policies—LIFO, FIFO, Grouping concept, units of issue item vs. bulk control.
7. Documentation—Forms/procedures, bin card.

8. Stores accounting system—FIFO, LIFO, Arrival cost, Standard cost.
9. Physical stock verification—need method-periodic, Perpetual, low inventory method, how to handle discrepancy report—ungust by inspection.

Physical stock verification (stock verification)

Need and Rationale

No matter how diligently a store keeper performs the custodial job or how carefully inventory records are maintained, some discrepancy between the actual and the book value of inventory is bound to occur. Systems are operated by people and people can make mistakes. For this reason every inventory item should be physically counted, measured or weighed and checked against book balance at least once a year. Thus physical stock verification is a systematic process with the following objectives:

1. To reconcile the book records and documents for their accuracy and usefulness.
2. To identify the areas which require more disciplined documentation control.
3. To back up the balance sheet stock figures.
4. To minimize pilferage and fraudulent practices.
5. Suggest preventive and corrective follow up measures.

Who Does It

Normally material audit or internal audit. One person is given exclusive responsibility and authority.

Process of Verification

1. Most involve stores people who know the physical location and can advise on the right method of measurement.
2. Must rectify omissions by discussion before reporting. Major discrepancies be re-verified.

Possible Source of Discrepancy

1. Large scale pilferage. It may be true for valuable items in short supply in the market due to lack of security check.
2. Wrong posting of records.
3. Loose documents control.
4. Evaporation losses due to poor storage method.

Discrepancy Voucher

It should provide relevant information such as date of verification, Part No/description/ code of location/quantity on records/in actual stock/discrepancy in units and in value terms. Whether surplus/deficit authenticated/approved by the concerned authority.

Table 5.1. Material Requisition

MATERIAL REQUISITION

Material required for —————— No ————

(Job or Process)

Department —————— Date ————

Sr. No.	Description	Code No.	Quantity		Rate	Amount	Entered on store register
			Demanded	Supplied			Page No.

Requisitioned by	Approved by	Material issued by	Received by
....	....	....	....

Table 5.2. Bin or Stock Card

BIN CARD

Bin No. ———— Maximum Quantity ————

Material code No. ———— Ordering Level ————

Stores Ledger No. ———— Minimum Quantity ————

Date	Quantity Received	Quantity Issued	Balance	Remarks

Table 5.3. Final Goods Inward Note (G.I. Note)

Material Port No. :		Serial No. :
Description :		
P.O. Reference :		
Carrier details	Supplier details	Inspection Report
Truck/Wagon	Supplier code	Test Results
R/R. Consignment note	Supplier name	Conclusions
Quantity received	________	Damage/Shortage
Quantity accepted	________	Shortage claim ref.
Quantity rejected	________	
Sd/-	Sd/-	Sd/-
Central Receiving Section	Inspection Department	Stores Department
Date :	Date :	Date :

Copies to: Accounts : Attention bills/Insurance and claims
Indentor : For Information
Materials : For Updating and expediting
Management Dept :
Stores : For stock records and reference

Storage Systems

Table 5.4. Stores System

Documents	*Activity*	*Documents*
Unloading Unpacking	Materials in Trucks, Wagons, etc, report at central receiving section	1. Identify the cargo and consignment by means of P.O. and delivery advice. 2. Check for damages, arrange for ODCs.
Inspection Metallurgical tests	Materials Reports to Stores for further inspection	3. Weighbridge checking with P.O. terms or country or measuring 4. Issue gate pass for the carrier to go to stores.
	Accepted materials Report back to stores Rejected materials Await processing Or dispatch to supplier	Rejection advice to supplier Preparation of G.I. Notes Advice to A/C, materials management for payment, deduction, deduction and ordering

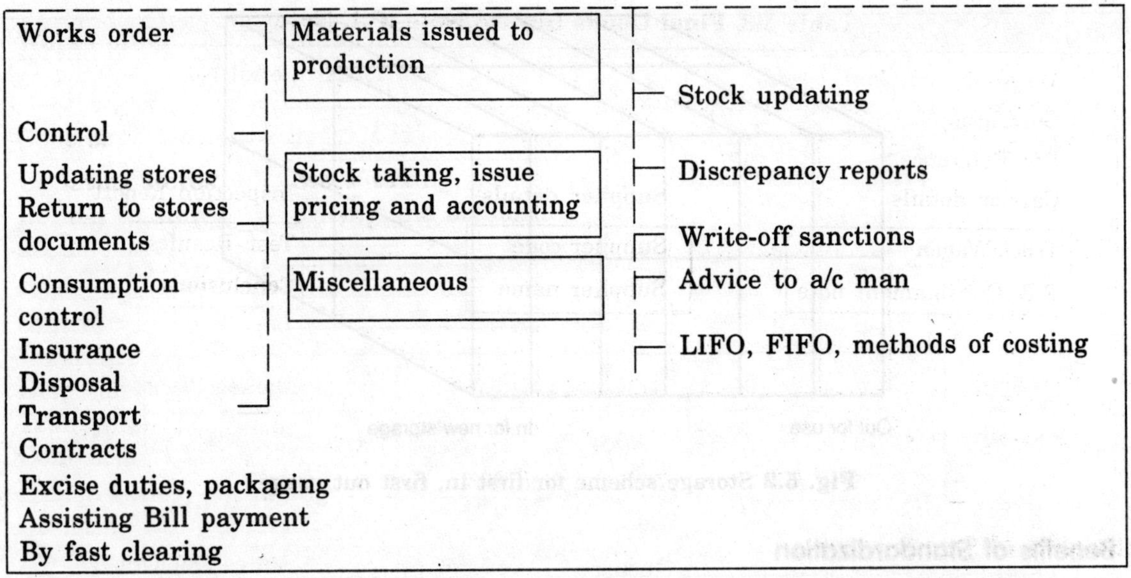

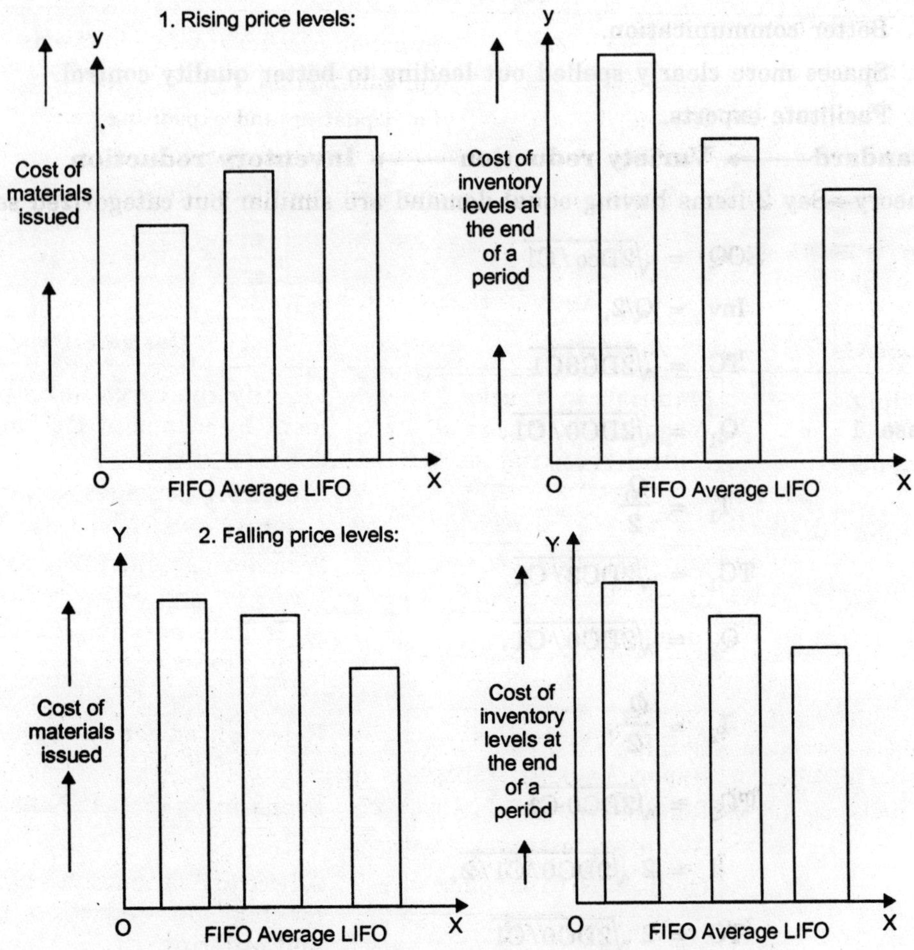

Fig. 5.1 Comparison of stores accounting systems

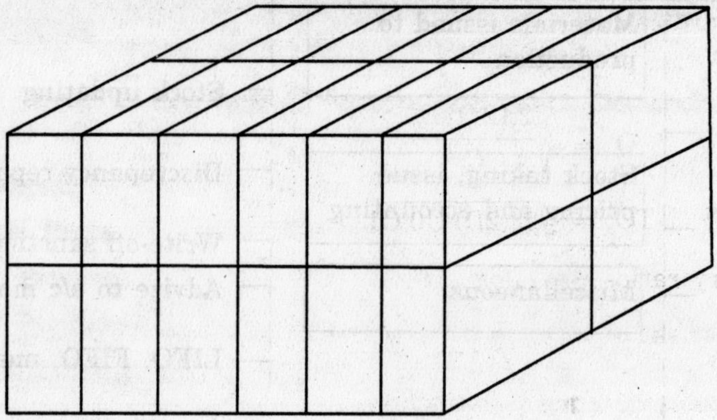

Fig. 5.2 Storage scheme for first in, first out usage

Benefits of Standardization

1. Helps reduction in inventory.
2. Better communication.
3. Spaces more clearly spelled out leading to better quality control.
4. Facilitate exports.

Standard ⟶ Variety reduction ⟶ Inventory reduction

Theory—Say 2 items having equal demand are similiar but categorized separately.

$$EOQ = \sqrt{2Dco / C1}$$

$$Inv = Q/2,$$

$$TC = \sqrt{2DC3C1}$$

Case. 1

$$Q_1 = \sqrt{2DC0/C1},$$

$$I_1 = \frac{Q_1}{2}$$

$$TC_1 = \sqrt{2DC3/C1}$$

$$Q_2 = \sqrt{2DC0/C1},$$

$$I_2 = \frac{Q_2}{2},$$

$$TC_2 = \sqrt{2DC0\ C1}$$

$$I = 2\ \sqrt{2DC0/C1/2},$$

$$TC = 2\ \sqrt{2DC0/C1}$$

After standardization:

$$D = 2D$$

$$Q = \sqrt{\frac{2.(2D).C_0}{C_1}}$$

$$TC = \sqrt{2.(2D)\, C0\, C1}$$

$$\text{Inventory ratio} = 1/\sqrt{2},$$

$$\text{Cost ratio} = 1/\sqrt{2}$$

Quantitative Benefits of Variety Reduction

Let n items be simplified into one due to standardization and codification. Let the requirement of these items be the same.

Case.1 When n items are separately stocked

$$Q_i = \sqrt{2RC_3C_1} \quad \text{for each item}$$

Average inventory for entire n items

$$= \sum_{i=1}^{n} \frac{Q_1}{2}$$

Total system cost for all items

$$= \sum_{i=1}^{n} \sqrt{\frac{2R\,C_3\,C_1}{i}}$$

$$= n\sqrt{2.RC1C3}$$

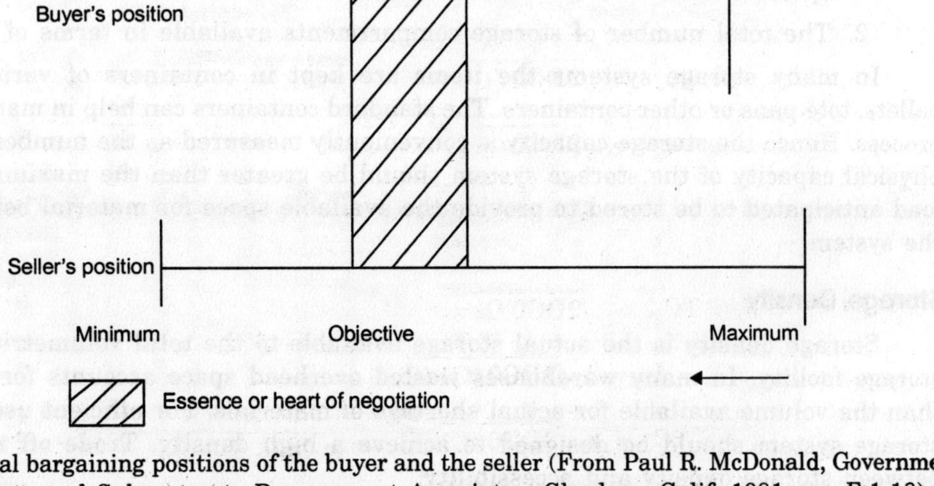

Fig. 5.3 Typical bargaining positions of the buyer and the seller (From Paul R. McDonald, Government Prime Contracts and Subcontracts Procurement Associates, Glerdora, Calif, 1981, pp. F-1-18)

5.2 STORAGE SYSTEMS

Types of Material Stored in any type of Factory and which Depends on the type of Business

1. Raw Material.
2. Purchased Parts.
3. Work in Process.
4. Finished Products.
5. Rework and Scrap.
6. Re-Use.
7. Tooling.
8. Spare Parts.
9. Office Supplies.
10. Plant Record.

Storage System Performance

The performance of the storing system must ensure that the items are kept in such a way that the investment made for the purpose of storage can be recovered as the organization are spending a lot for the safety of the materials. There must be some measures to be used to assess the performance of storage systems such as:

1. Storage Capacity.
2. Density.
3. Accessibility.
4. Throughput.

In addition to the above, the other factors may be considered like utilization and reliability. **The Storage capacity can be Measured in two ways:**

1. The total space available like length, breadth and height *i.e.*, total volume of space.
2. The total number of storage compartments available in terms of load/items.

In many storage systems the items are kept in containers of various sizes like pallets, tote pans or other containers .The standard containers can help in material handling process. Hence the storage capacity is conveniently measured as the number of loads. The physical capacity of the storage system should be greater than the maximum number of load anticipated to be stored to provide the available space for material being entered in the system.

Storage Density

Storage density is the actual storage available to the total volumetric space in the storage facility. In many warehouses wasted overhead space accounts for more volume than the volume available for actual shortage of materials. For efficient use of space, the storage system should be designed to achieve a high density. Trade off must be made between storage density and accessibility.

Storage throughput is defined as the hourly rate at which the storage system

1. receives and puts loads into storage system.
2. retrieves and delivers loads to the output station.

In many factories and warehouses operations in some of the days the required rate of storage/retrieval transactions is greater than other times. Storage transaction consists of the following elements:

1. Pick up load at input station.
2. Travel to storage location.
3. Place load into storage location.
4. Travel back to input station.

Retrieval Transaction Consists of

1. Travel to storage location.
2. Pick items from storage.
3. Travel to output station.
4. Unload at output station.

Utilization is defined as the proportion of time that the system is actually being used for performing storage and retrieval operations compared with the time it is available. Utilization varies depending on the work and changes from hour to hour. It is desirable to design an automated storage system for relatively high utilization, in the range of 80-90%. The factors which affect the utilization are:

1. If utilization is too low then the system is probably over-designed.
2. If the utilization is too high, then there is no allowance for rush periods or systems breakdowns.

Availability is a measure of system reliability defined as the proportion of time that the system is capable of operating compared with normal scheduled shift hours.

5.3 STORAGE LOCATION STRATEGIES

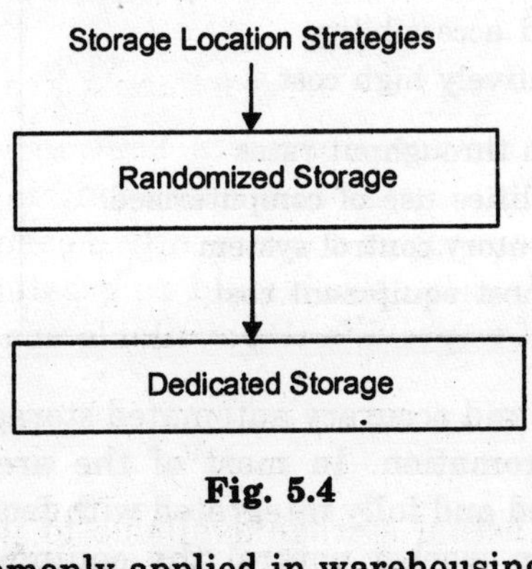

Fig. 5.4

These strategies are commonly applied in warehousing operations. Each item stored in warehouse is known as Stock Keeping Unit (SKU). The SKU uniquely identifies the type of item. *In randomized storage,* items are stored in any available location in the storage system. When an order is received for a given SKU, the stock is retrieved from storage according to a first in first out policy so that the item held in storage the longest are used to make up order.

In dedicated storage, SKUs are assigned to specific locations in the storage facility. This means that locations are reserved for all SKU stored in the system and so the number of storage locations for each SKU must be sufficient to accommodate its maximum inventory level. There are some bases for specifying the storage locations.

1. The items are stored in part number or product sequence or as per the need in case of emergency.
2. Items are stored according to activity level.
3. Items are stored according to their activity to space ratio, the higher ratio being located closer to the input/output station.

5.4 CONVENTIONAL STORAGE METHODS AND EQUIPMENTS

There are various methods available for storage and it depends on the type of material to be stored. The application characteristics and storage methods are given as under.

Table. 5.5 Bulk Storage Refers to the Storage of Stock in an Open Floor Area

Storage Equipment	*Advantages & Disadvantages*	*Application*
Bulk Storage	High Density is possible Low accessibility Lowest possible cost per sq. ft.	Storage of low turnover Large stock/large unit load
Rack System	Low cost Good storage density Good accessibility	Palletized loads in warehouses
Shelves and bins	Some stock items not clearly visible	Storage of individual Items on shelves
Drawer Storage	Contents of drawer easily visible Good accessibility Relatively high cost	Small tools Small stock items Repair parts
Automated storage system	High throughput rates Facilities use of computerized Inventory control system Highest equipment cost	Work in process storage Order picking

For the purpose of speed and accuracy automated storage system is required. Different systems are available in automation. In most of the areas the operations are totally automated, computer controlled and fully integrated with factory and warehouse operations. At the other extreme, human worker control the equipment and perform the storage/ retrieval transactions.

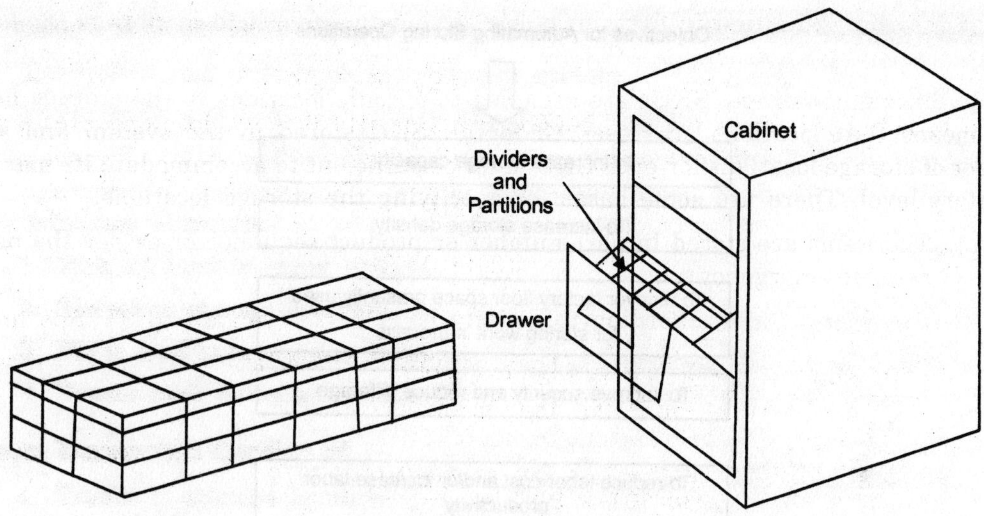

Fig. 5.5. Drawer storage

5.5 AUTOMATED STORAGE/RETRIEVAL SYSTEM

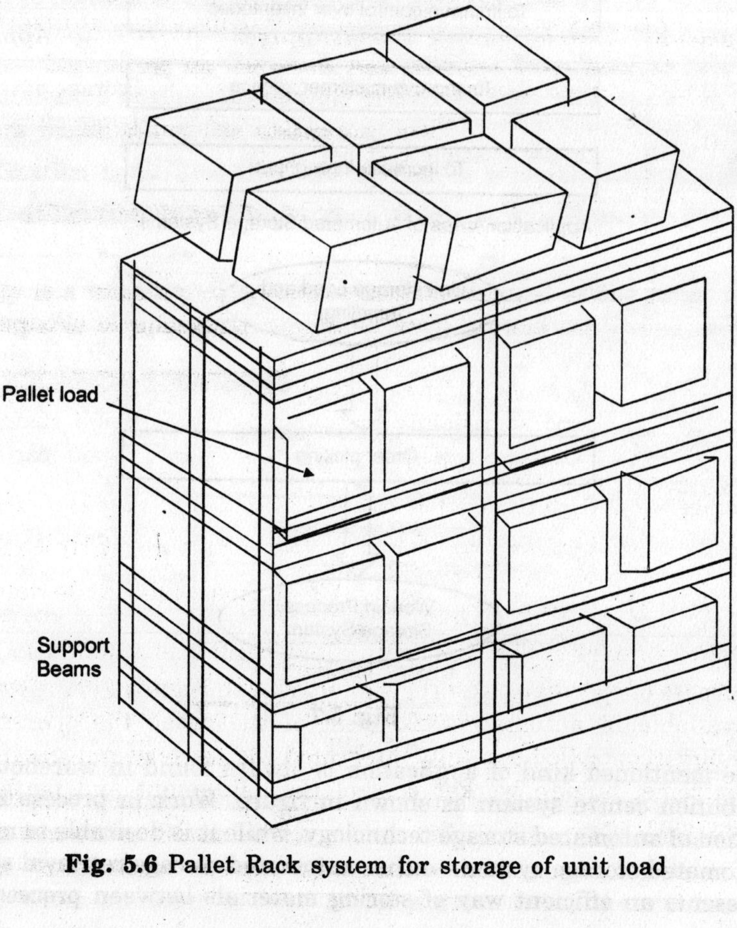

Fig. 5.6 Pallet Rack system for storage of unit load

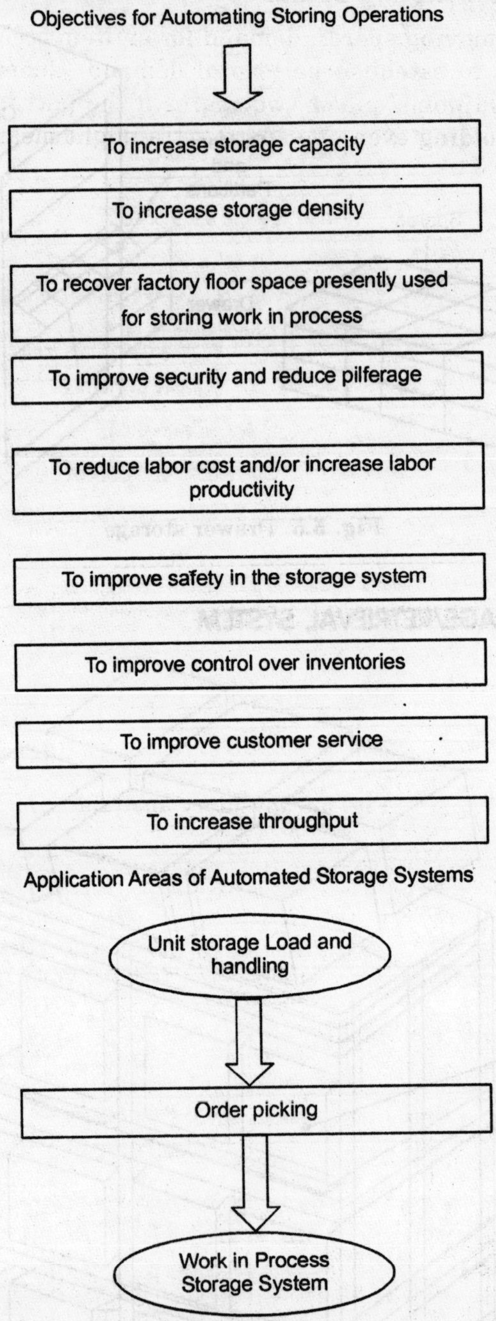

Fig. 5.7

The above mentioned kind of application is always found in warehousing for finished goods in distribution centre system as shown in figure. Work in process storage is a more recent application of automated storage technology, while it is desirable to minimize the work in process. Automated storage system—either automated storage/retrieval system or carousel systems—represents an efficient way of storing materials between processing steps.

Inventory Analysis of Slow Moving Spares

In the case of slow moving spares, demand for an item occurs occasionally and hence past records rarely help to establish pattern of demand. Generally the decision process examines whether to hold none, one or two spares if the part is an expensive one. If the part is expensive then holding even one spare extra might mean a significant blocking of capital.

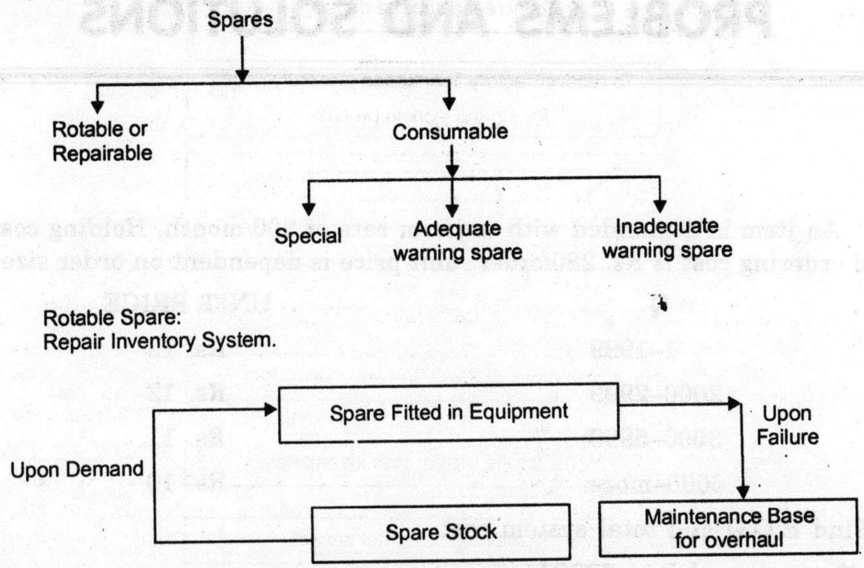

Fig. 5.8 Inventory analysis

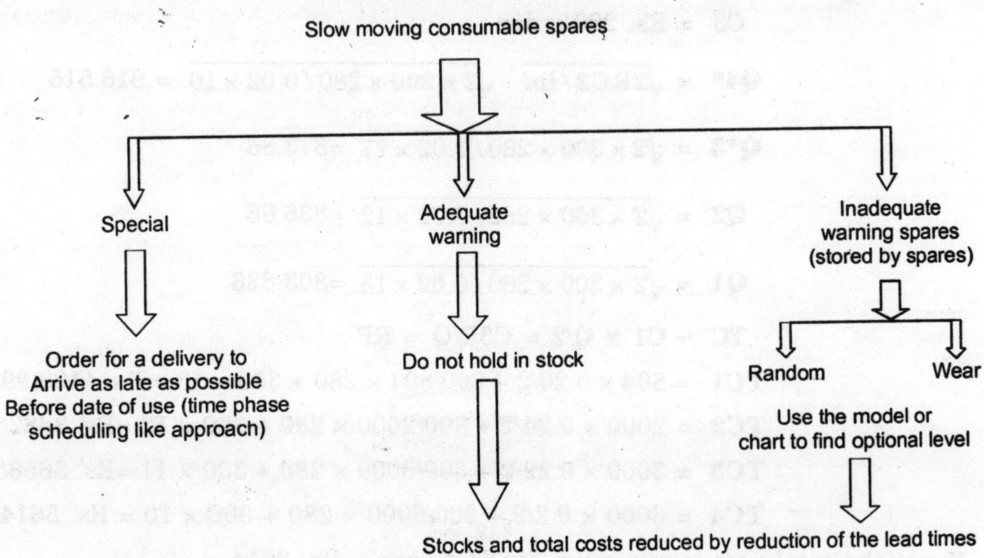

Fig. 5.9 Consumable spares

6

CHAPTER

PROBLEMS AND SOLUTIONS

Q.1. An item is demanded with uniform rate of 300/month. Holding cost is 2% per month and ordering cost is Rs. 280/order, unit price is dependent on order size as follows:

Q	UNIT PRICE
1–1999	Rs. 13
2000–2999	Rs. 12
3000–5999	Rs. 11
6000–more	Rs. 10

Find E.O.Q and total system cost.

Solution: R = 300/Month

C1 = IXPi = 0.02 × 10

C3 = Rs. 280/order

$$\mathbf{Q4^*} = \sqrt{2RC3/Ipi} \quad \sqrt{2 \times 300 \times 280/0.02 \times 10} = 916.515$$

$$\mathbf{Q^*3} = \sqrt{2 \times 300 \times 280/0.02 \times 11} = 873.86$$

$$\mathbf{Q2} = \sqrt{2 \times 300 \times 280/0.02 \times 12} = 836.66$$

$$\mathbf{Q1} = \sqrt{2 \times 300 \times 280/0.02 \times 13} = 803.836$$

TC = C1 × Q/2 = C3R/Q = RP

TC1 = 804 × 0.26/2 + 300/804 × 280 + 300 × 13 = Rs. 4108.99/month

TC2 = 2000 × 0.24/2 + 300/2000 × 280 + 300 × 12 =Rs. 3882/month.

TC3 = 3000 × 0.22/2 + 300/3000 × 280 + 300 × 11 =Rs. 3658/month.

TC4 = 6000 × 0.2/2 + 300/6000 × 280 + 300 × 10 = Rs. 3614/month

Hence the total cost is minimum for TC4 case = Rs. 3614

Order size = 6000 or above is economical.

Q.2. An item is demanded with uniform rate of 25000/year. Carrying cost is Rs. 2.5 per unit/year, and ordering cost is Rs. 100/order. Purchasing price is Rs. 30 per unit. The supplier offer a discount of 1% on purchasing price if the item is ordered in a lot of 5000, and 1.5% if the item is ordered in a lot of 10,000. Find the EOQ and total system cost.

Solution: Demand R = 25000/year

Carrying cost C1 = 2.5/unit/year

Ordering cost = Rs. 100/order

Purchase Price = P = Rs. 30/unit

Discount of 1% P E 5000.

Discount of 1.5% P E 10,000

$$\text{EOQ} = \sqrt{2RC3/C1} = \sqrt{2 \times 25000 \times 100/2.5} = 1414.2$$

Total Cost = C1.Q/2 + C3R/Q + PR

= 2.5 × 1414.2/2 + 100 × 25000/1414.2 + 30 × 25000

= 2.5 × 707.1 + 100 × 17.67 + 750000

= 1767.75 + 1767 + 750000

= **753534.75**

For 10% Discount 30 × 1% = 0.3

30–0.3 = 29.7

Rs. 29.7

2.5 × 1414.2/2 + 100 × 25000/1414.2 + 29.70 × 25000

= 1767.75 + 1767 + 675000

= **Rs. 749250**

Q = 10000 Discount 1.5% P 29.55

TC (10000,29.55)

10000/2 × 2.5 + 25000/10000 × 100 + 25000 × 29.55

= **751500**

Hence TC (5000, 29.77) = Rs. **749250**

Q.3. An item is demanded at the rate of 200 units/month. The supplier is able to supply at the rate of 500 units/months. The item costs Rs. 1500 per unit and unit carrying charge is 25% per year. Ordering cost is Rs 400 per order and shortages can be backlogged at a cost of Rs. 500 per unit short per month.

(*a*) Determine optimal values of order quantity, maximum stock level and total system cost.

(*b*) If backlogging is not allowed and supplier is instantaneous, what impact does it make on total cost.

(*c*) In (*b*) above, if % cost increase over optimum is permissible, what optimal range of EOQ is obtained.

Solution: Backlogged cost

C2 = Rs. 500/unit/month

C1 = Cost of carrying = 0.25 × 1500 = Rs. 375

C2 = 500

C3 = 400 = Ordering cost

Procurement cost = P = 500 × 12 = 6000 units

Item demanded = R = 200 × 12 = 2400 units

Optimal values economic ordering cost

$$Q^* = \sqrt{2RC3/C1(1-R/P)} \times \sqrt{C1+C2/C2}$$

$$= \sqrt{\frac{2 \times 2400 \times 400}{375 \times \left(1-\frac{2400}{6000}\right)}} \times \sqrt{\frac{375+500 \times 12}{500 \times 12}} = 95.2$$

Total cost $= TC^* = \sqrt{2RC3C1(1-R/P)} \times \sqrt{C2/C1+C2}$

$$= \sqrt{2 \times 2400 \times 400 \times 375 \times \left(1-\frac{2400}{6000}\right)} \times \sqrt{\frac{300 \times 12}{375+500 \times 12}} = 20164.03$$

Maximum Stock Level

$$S^* = \sqrt{\frac{2RC3}{C1\left(1-\frac{R}{P}\right)}} \times \sqrt{\frac{C2}{C1+C2}}$$

$$= \sqrt{2 \times 2400 \times 400 \times 375 \times \left(1-\frac{2400}{6000}\right)} \times \sqrt{\frac{500 \times 12}{375+500 \times 12}}$$

$= 69.47 \cong 70 \times 1.21 = 90.36$

B-Backlogging is not allowed C2 $\longrightarrow p \to \infty$

Total cost $TC = \sqrt{2RC3C1(1-R/P)}$

$$= \sqrt{2 \times 2400 \times 400 \times 375(1-2400/6000)}$$

= Rs. 20784.60

Backlogged is not allowed as the total cost is increased.

C – TC New = 1.01TC old

$$\frac{TC'}{TC} = 1.01 = \frac{1+b^2}{2b^2}$$

$b^2 - 2.02b + 1 = 0$

$b = 2.02 \pm \sqrt{(2.02)^2 - 4/2}$

$b = 1.15, 0.87$

Q.4. Following four items are procured from the same vendor.

Item	*Monthly Demand*	*Unit Price*
1	200	Rs. 10
2	1400	Rs. 25
3	3000	Rs. 15
4	1500	Rs. 40

Fraction of carrying charge is 24% per year and ordering cost is Rs. 900 per order. Find optimal decision variables and total system cost of a joint replenishment policy. What cost increase will result if items were procured independently.

Solution: C3 = 900

$$C1 = 0.24 \times 10 = 2.4 \times 12$$

$$R = 200 \times 12$$

$$TC1 = \sqrt{2RC3C1}$$

$$= \sqrt{2 \times 200 \times 12 \times 900 \times 2.4 \times 12}$$

$$= 11154.19$$

$$TC2 = \sqrt{2RC3C1}$$

$$= \sqrt{2 \times 1400 \times 900 \times 25 \times 12 \times 0.24 \times 12}$$

$$= 13469.96 \times 3.464 = 46661.31$$

$$TC3 = \sqrt{2 \times 3000 \times 12 \times 900 \times 15 \times 12 \times 0.24}$$

$$= 52908.97$$

$$TC4 = \sqrt{2 \times 1500 \times 12 \times 900 \times 40 \times 0.24 \times 12}$$

$$= 61094.025$$

$$TC = TC1 + TC2 + TC3 + TC4$$

$$= 11154.16 + 46661.31 + 52908.97 + 61094.025$$

$$= \text{Rs. } 171818.46$$

$$TC = \sqrt{2C3\ \Sigma\ RiCi}$$

$$= \frac{\sqrt{2 \times 900 \times [200 \times 12 \times 10 \times 12 \times 0.24 + 1400 \times 12 \times 25 \times 0.24 \times 12 +}}{\sqrt{3000 \times 12 \times 15 \times 0.24 \times 12 + 1500 \times 12 \times 40 \times 0.24 \times 12]}}$$

$$= \text{Rs. } 91641.03$$

$$Qi = \sqrt{2C3 / \Sigma Ri\ Cii}$$

$$Qi = 200 \times 12 \sqrt{2 \times 900 / 4665600} = 47.14$$

$$Q2 = 1400 \times 12 \times 0.0196 = 329.98$$

$$Q3 = 3000 \times 12 \times 0.0116 = 707.10$$

$$Q4 = 1500 \times 12 \times 0.0190 = 353.55$$

Q.5. You have to supply your customer with 100 units of a certain product every Monday (and only then) you obtain the product from a local supplier at Rs. 60/unit. The cost of carrying inventory is estimated at 15% per year of the cost of products carried. The costs of ordering and transportation from the supplier are Rs. 150 per year.

(*a*) Describe graphically the inventory system.

(*b*) Find EOQ and total cost.

Soluton: Cost of carrying

Ordering cost $= C3 = 150/\text{year}$

Annual demand $R = 52 \times 100 = 5200$ units

$C1 = 15\%$ per year

$0.15 \times 60 = $ Rs. 9/-

$$EOQ^* = \sqrt{2RC3/C1} = \sqrt{2 \times 5200 \times 150/9} = 416.33$$

Total cost $$TC^* = \sqrt{2RC1C3} = \sqrt{2 \times 5200 \times 150 \times 9}$$

$$= 3746.99 = \text{Rs. } 3747.00$$

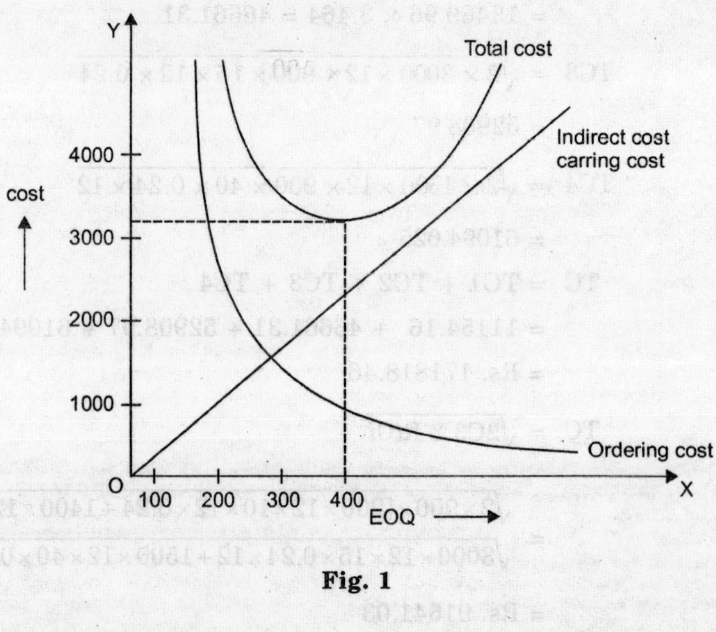

Fig. 1

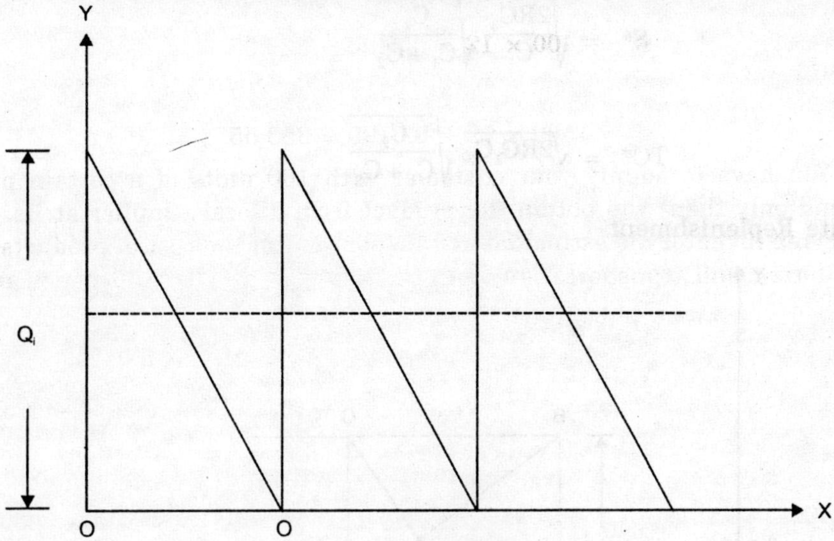

Fig. 2

Total cycle cost

$$\text{Minimize } N = \sum \frac{Di}{Qi} \; e_2 \rightarrow \alpha$$

$$\text{(TCS) } N = \text{Constant } \frac{1}{2}\left(\Sigma\sqrt{DiVi}\right)^2$$

Planned Back logging

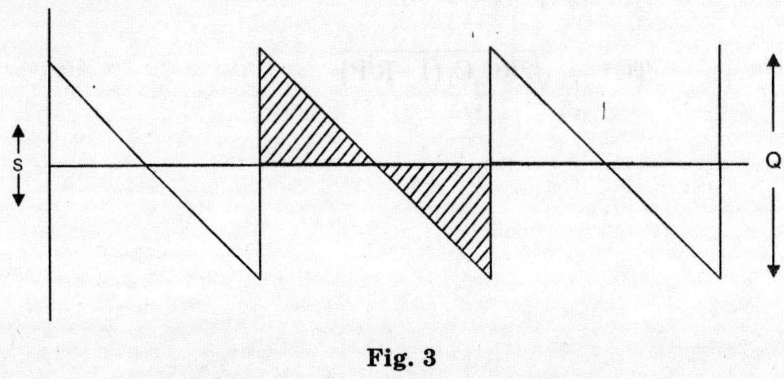

Fig. 3

$$\frac{t_2}{t_1} = \frac{Q-S}{Q}$$

$$Q^* = \sqrt{\frac{2RC_3}{C_1}}\sqrt{\frac{C_1+C_2}{C_2}}$$

$$S^* = \sqrt{\frac{2RC_3}{C_1}}\sqrt{\frac{C_2}{C_1 + C_2}}$$

$$TC^* = \sqrt{2RC_1C_3}\sqrt{\frac{C_2}{C_1 + C_2}}$$

Finite Replenishment

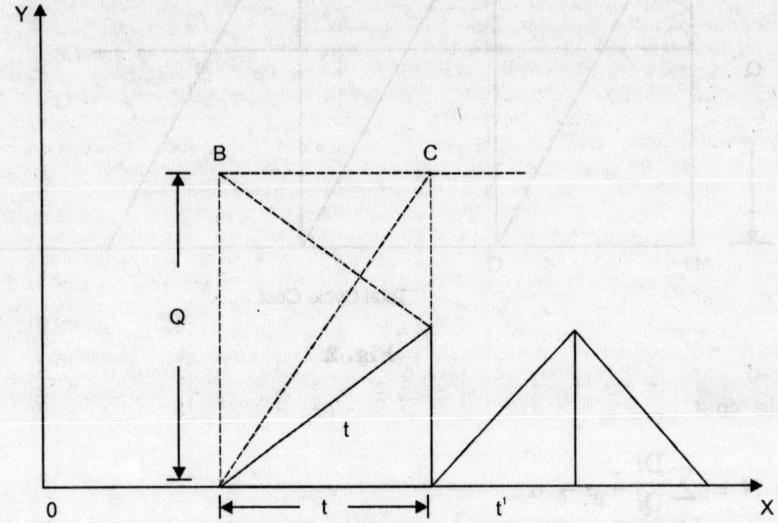

Fig. 4

$$Q^* = \sqrt{\frac{2RC_3}{C_1(1 - R/P)}}$$

$$TC^* = \sqrt{2RC_3C_1(1 - R/P)}$$

Time and Motion Study

CHAPTER 7

INDUSTRIAL ENGINEERING

7.1 PROCESS OF CONVERSION

INPUT ⟶ METHOD STUDY ⟶ OUTPUT

Man
Machine
Material
Money

Fig. 7.1

Cost and Time

1. Reduction in cost—reduction in time
2. Increased productivity
3. Effective utilization of resources
4. Effective and safe use of manpower (Lesser fatigue to the workers)

Industrial Engineering is concerned with design improvement and installation of the integrated system of man, material and equipment. It draws upon specialize knowledge and skill of the mathematical, physical and social science together with the principle and method of engineering analysis and design to specify, predict and evaluate the results to be obtained from such system.

7.2 DESIGN OF PHYSICAL PRODUCTION FACILITIES

1. Specification of basic methods of conversion of manufacturing engineering
2. Specification of flow of materials (Materials Management handling)
3. Specified work methods basically deal with the purpose of integration of human operations into production methods
   (*a*) Design of work method engineering.
   (*b*) Specification of performance and time.
   (*c*) Design of system (Integration of human beings).

Design of Operating System

(*a*) Production time and control.

(*b*) Sales.

Maynard defines techniques of study as the engineering approach applied to all the factors including that of human factors involved in the production and distribution of product as such. He further emphasizes that this engineering approach based on systematic approach, *i.e.*, scientific management and its various principles given by the Taylor.

Taylor defines the scientific management as the application of science and scientific methods for the management of any industrial or commercial concern so as to secure maximum prosperity of both employees and employer.

Scientific management is the system of management in which science replaces rule of thumb, escort maximum output replaces restricted output, and thus there is development of each and every man to get his efficiency and prosperity.

Four Essential Factors

1. Development of science for each element of mans work must methods have a proper and standardize sequence method conuersion.
2. Scientific selection training and development of each work.
3. Friendly cooperation between management and workers to do the work in accordance with the developed science or agreed method.
4. Equal share of work between management and workers.

Resources

Man	Machine	Material	Service	Plant and Machine Equipment

↓

The Management to obtain Facts
Plans, Directs, Coordinates, Controls
Motivates in order to produce

↓

Goods & Services

↓

Products

Fig. 7.2

7.3 METHOD STUDY

Method study is the systematic recording and critical examination of existing and proposed ways of doing work as a means of developing and applying easier and more effective methods and reducing costs.

Work measurement is the application of techniques assigned to establish the time for a qualified worker to carry out a specific job at a defined level of performance.

Work study is defined as the scientific study and analysis of resources used in the performance activity. It is the analysis of the methods of materials and of tools and equipment used or to be used in the performance of any activity. This analysis is carried out with the following purposes:

1. Developing the most economical method of work
2. Standardizing the materials tools
3. Accurate method determine the time required to carry out the process of conversion.
4. Assess the worker's work and develop and integrate into the system.

Work Study is a generic term for those techniques, particularly for method study and work measurement, which are used in the examination of human work in all its contexts and which lead systematically to the investigation of all the factors which affect the efficiency and economy of the situation being reviewed in order to effect improvement.

7.4 BASIC PROCEDURE OF WORK STUDY

There are *eight steps in performing the work study.* They are :

Select, Record, Examine, Develop, Measure, Define, Install and Maintain.

1. Select the job or the process to be studied.
2. Record from direct observations every thing that happens using the most suitable of the recording techniques so that the data will be in the most convenient form to be analyzed.
3. Examine the recorded facts critically and challenge every thing that is done considering in turn the purpose of the activity, the place where it is performed, the sequence in which it is done, the person who is doing it, the means by which it is done.
4. Develop the most economic method taking into account all the circumstances.
5. Measure the quantity of work involved in the method selected and calculate the standard time for doing it.
6. Define the new method and related time so that it can always be identified.
7. Install the new method as agreed standard practice with the time allowed.
8. Maintain the new standard practice by proper control procedures.

7.5 RECORDING TECHNIQUES

Record in a compact and graphical method so that the information can be made available easily and effectively during the critical examination. The various recording techniques can be classified as under:

Table 7.1 Recording Techniques

Process Chart	Diagram	Models	Photograph Aids
*-Out Line Process Chart.	*-Flow Diagram	*Two Dimensional	*Skill Photograph.
(O.P.C)	(Line)	*Three Dimensional	* Movie.
*-Operation Process Chart.	*-String Diagram		*Narrow Motion
(OP.PC)	Two Dimensional		(continuous)
	and		*Continuous
	Three Dimensional		Micro Motion
*Multiple Activity chart			
	Flow Process Chart		
*Two Handed Process chart	* Man		
	*Machine		
*Travel Chart	*Material		
	*Combined		
*SIMO Chart			

7.6 PROCESS CHART

It is a graphical representation of the sequence of the events which occur in the performance of any activity and this graphical representation is done by the use of various symbols that is why it is called graphical.

Construction of Process Chart

A. Information Section

B. Main Body

C. Summary Section

Types of Process Chart

Outline Process Chart.

(Existing Method).

Nature of Activity.

Manufacturing/Assembly.

Beginning of Activity.

Extension of Activity C1.

Time of Performance.

Distance Moved.

Name of Worker.

Name Of Recorder.

Date Of Occurrence.

Workplace Layout.

Flow Process Chart

Complete sequence of flow of work in terms of man/machine/material

Two handed process records the movement of the two moveable parts in a synchronized manner, *i.e.,* left hand right hand chart.

Recording activity of repetitive operation in which we are interested to find out the movement of the two hand and idleness of the one hand in the beginning or end is shown as temporary delay. It is part of Motion Study.

Outline Process Chart (O.P.U)—(Overall picture of sequence of operation which takes place, *i.e.,* occurrence of events).

Operation Process Chart—(In summary of chart that is for management is given overall picture of the process).

Gantt Chart—When two or more activities recorded are called Gantt Chart. (To study to analyze the relationship with different subjects for the purpose of organizing activity, finding out how many machines are loaded and unloaded etc. Finding out of the % for different aspects.

Travel Chart—Movement of different subjects within the department or outside department). How the material moves from one department to another. Basically a non productive time as it does not pushes the material from one station to another.

SIMO Chart—Detailed version of the two handed process chart in which we record the movement of two hands at Micro Level that is not the general movement recorded. It is basically used for carrying out the detailed motion study.

7.7 STRING DIAGRAM

Threads are used for the study of the layout problem material handling problem how the matenal handling to be designed. Instead of using lines, threads can be used and measure the length of the threads in string diagram. Carried out at two or more than three floors is called three dimensional process.

String Diagram

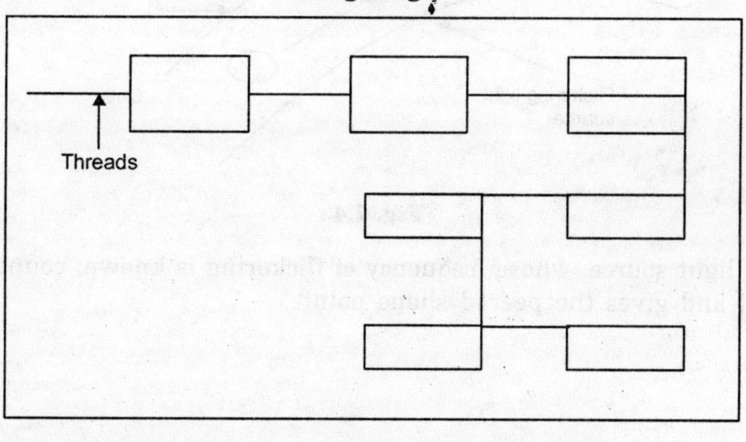

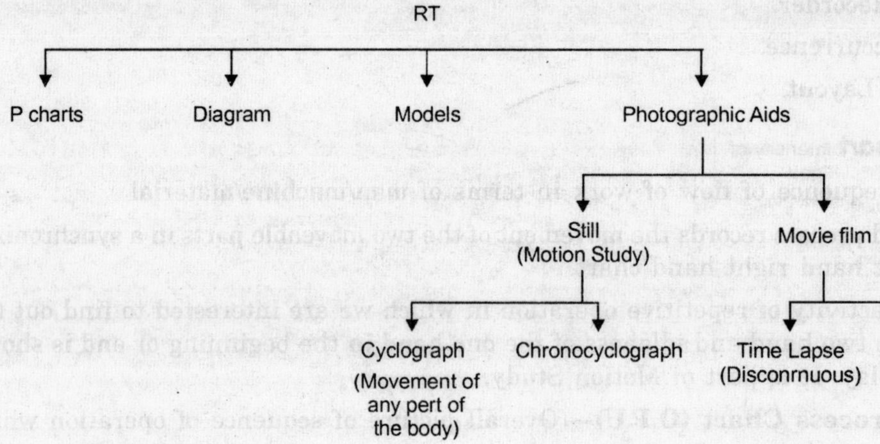

Fig. 7.3

Filming Total Process, SIMO Chart, Frame by Frame Analysis, Two Handed Process Chart, Higher Class of Motion.

1. **Motion confined to movement of Figuers—Knuckle**
2. **Motion confined to Figuers, Wrist—Hands**
3. **Motion confined to F + W + Lower Arm—Elbow**
4. **Motion confined to F + W + LA + Upper Arm—Shoulder**
5. **Motion confined to F + Wrist + LA + UA + Shoulder—Torso**

* **Continuous film Phenomenon > 16 times/sec,**
* **Movie film at 960 frame**
* **Ordinary video film 1080 frame/sec. Any manual work can be synthesise the basic motion and it is performed under certain condition that is 17 therbligs.**

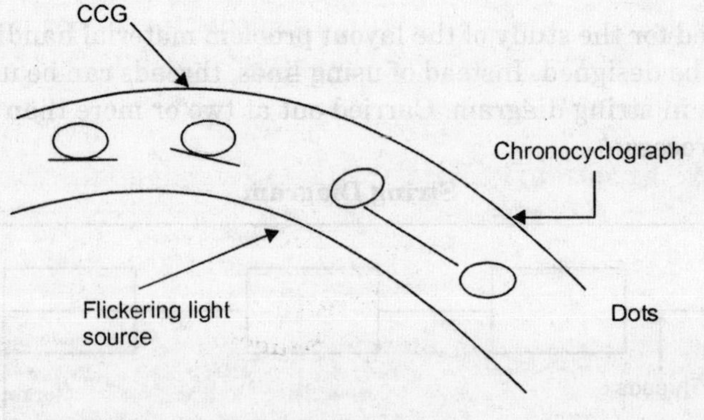

Fig. 7.4

Flickering light source, whose frequency of flickering is known, counts the dots (get the time taken) and gives the peered shape point.

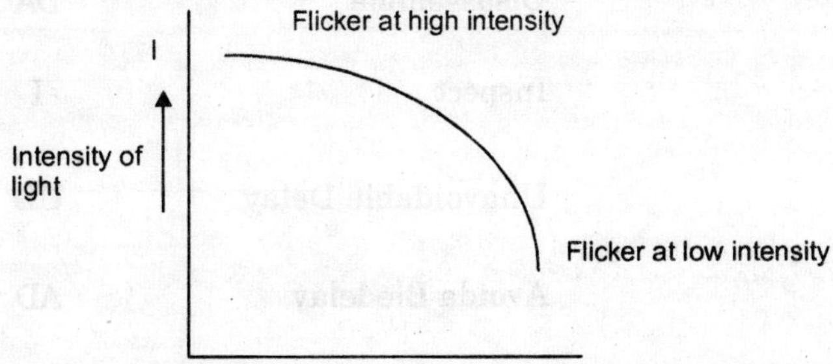

Fig. 7.5 Analysing the motion and analyzing the movement etc.

Basic elementary motion and that motion cannot be further subdivided.

Sampling Process is a regular time lapse : one frame and then gap and then frame and take a film etc.

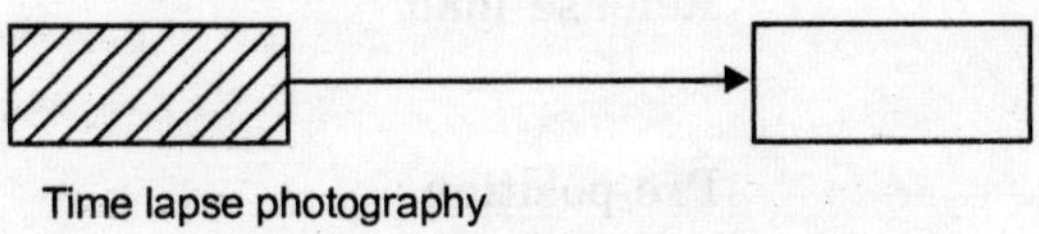

Fig. 7.6 Discontinuons film process

Instead of recording 960 frame we can record upto 120 frame/sec. Movie camera shutter is always open 15-120 frames/minutes *i.e.,* every 4 seconds.15-30, 60, 120 frame/sec.

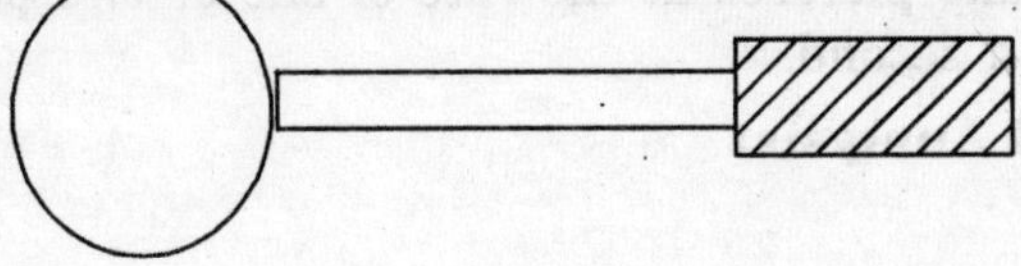

Fig. 7.7 Memo motion study

7.8 MICROMOTION STUDY

Therbligs

Symbol	**Name**	**Abbreviation**
	Search	sh
	Find	F
	Select	st
	Grasp	Gp
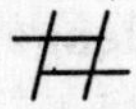	Assemble	A

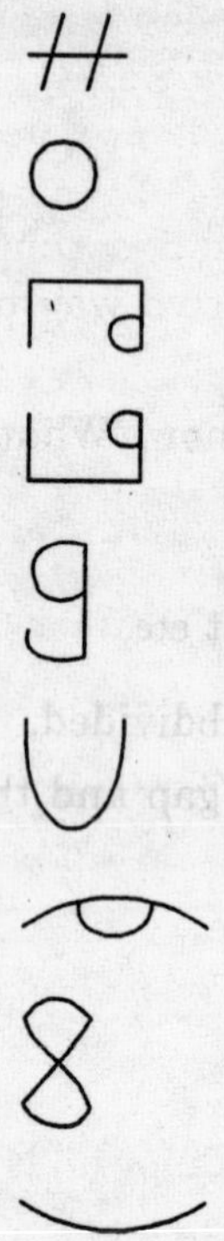

Disassemble	DA
Inspect	I
Unavoidable Delay	UD
Avoida Bledelay	AD
Position	β
Use	U
Release load	RL
Pre-position	PP
Transport Empty	TE

Memo motion Photography—A form of time lapse photography which records activity by a cine camera adapted to take pictures at longer intervals than normal. The time interval usually lies between ½ second. A camera is placed with a view over the whole working area to take pictures at the rate of one or two per second instead of the usual rate of 24 frames a second.

Examine (Critical Analysis)

S-Select

R-Record

E-Examine or Analysis

Existence of non productive activity to be minimized

○

□

⇨

D

▽

1. Make Ready Activities 2. Do Activities 3. Put away activity

Out of the above one we call as Productive. Non Productive (Elimination etc. are Non Productive), *i.e.*, D, increases the % of Productive activity. We challenge by means of putting a symmetric questionnaire to find out the necessity. Develop a sequence of productive activities. It is the analysis of the facts and information which we have collected by means of recording techniques, by means of challenge the very existence of each and every part of the problem. The problem consists of five things including Purpose, Place, Means, Person and Sequence. Using the techniques of elimination, minimization, simplification combination and rearrangement with a view to develop a more effective way of solving problem.

Rudy and Kipling—six honest serving men taught me all I know. What, Where, When, Who, How and Why.

First Purpose —— What
Place —— Where
Sequence/Time —— When
Person —— Who
Means —— How

7.9 PROCEDURE STAGES

1. Primary (Stage) Questions———YES, NO, WHY
2. Secondary (Stages)———To establish various alternatives if answer is NO.
3. Tertian Stage——— Evaluation of various alternatives; selection and development of most suitable alternative.

Primary Stage

YES ⟶ STOP If NO

PURPOSE —— WHAT is actually being done?
WHY is it necessary at all?
PLACE —— WHERE is it being done?
WHY there only?
SEQUENCE —— WHEN is it being done?
WHY then only?
PERSON —— WHO does it?
WHY that person only?
MEANS —— HOW is it being done?
WHY is it being done that way?

Secondary Stage

WHAT else could be done?
WHERE else could it be done?
WHEN else could it be done?
WHO else could do it?
HOW else could it be done?

Tertiary Stage

(Justification in terms of Physibility, Capacity, Restrictions etc.)

WHAT should be done?

WHERE should it be done?

WHEN should it be done?

WHO should do it?

HOW should it be done?

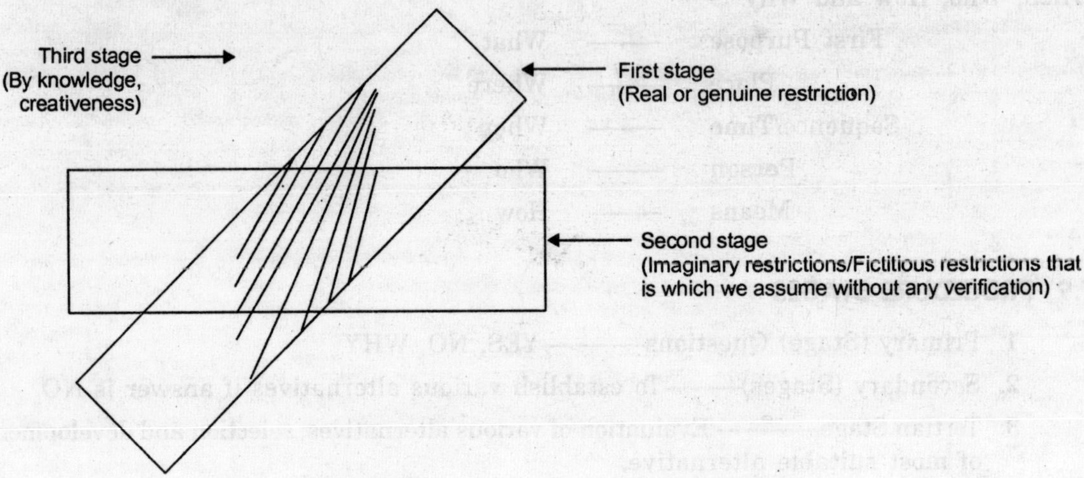

Fig. 7.8 Boundary constraints restrictions

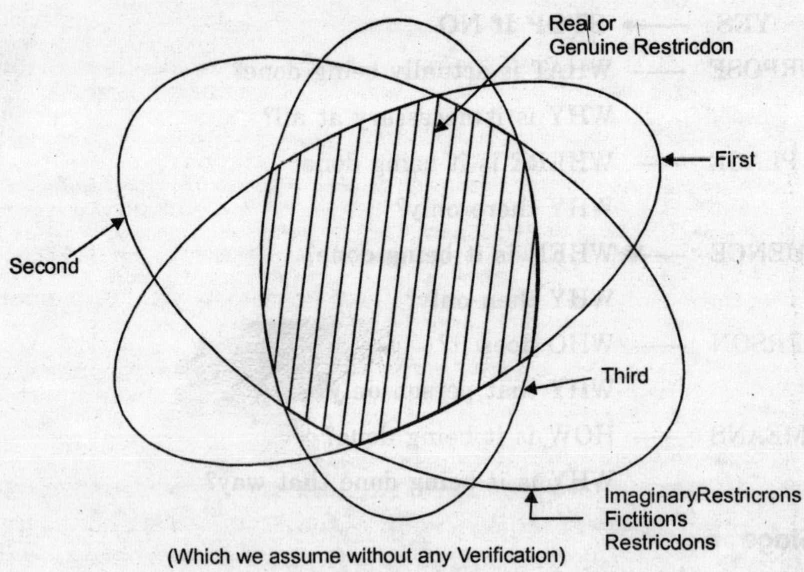

Fig. 7.8 (*a*)

Search for Alternatives—List out the various alternatives in case NO.

1. Brainstorming session (General Meeting)

2. Creativeness → Knowledge of people
   → Amount of interest, Aptitudes, Method used, Chances

Factors for Search of Alternatives

1. Exert necessary and all out effort.
2. Make liberal use of questioning aptitude.
3. Try always a systematic approach.
4. Seek as many as possible alternatives.
5. Never hesitate in consulting other people connected or not connected. The most important attempt to divert your attention from the existing solution is nearby. For all this try brainstorming and good discussions, avoid conjunction, avoid premature rejection and premature satisfaction or acceptance. Avoid all restrictions at the level of brainstorming. Test out and try even the most ridiculous ideas on work in an atmosphere of creativeness.

Evaluations of Alternatives

Usefulness of Constraints are → Real
→ Genuine
→ Imaginary
→ Knowledge of designs

Evaluation depends on main or key criteria on which the evaluation has to be carried out, *i.e.*, the process of judgment. Process of evaluation depends on economic, technical and numerical criteria; it may be initial cost, operating cost, performance criteria, appearance criteria etc.

7.10 FIVE STEPS INVOLVED IN THE PROCESS OF EVALUATIONS

1. Select the specific criterion (single criterion or more than single criterion may be used).
2. Predict the performance of each alternative with respect to each alternative.
3. Convert these estimated performance to some monetary value or some quantitative value.
4. Compare the alternatives on the basis of quantitative and unquantitative criterion and then select the alternative preferred or solution. (economic, technical, numerical)

The quantitative criteria which are basically economic criteria and two measurable factors are time taken in performance, the time required and the cost consideration.

The unquantitative criteria which in many of the situations are quite large in numbers that is fatigue gets developed. The quantitative terms 1-Time Taken (for the process of conversion), standard system for repeatable jobs time measurement.

Develop Framing of Different Proposals

1. List out the feasible alternatives on the basis of constraints.
2. Make and check the interlinks.

3. Evaluate these interlinks in terms of set criterion for comparison (Total time taken or total amount of cost involved).
4. Pick out the top three proposals.
5. Write down some summary details of these three proposals.
6. Consult people top, middle and workers level.
7. Write down the restrictions of preferred solutions.

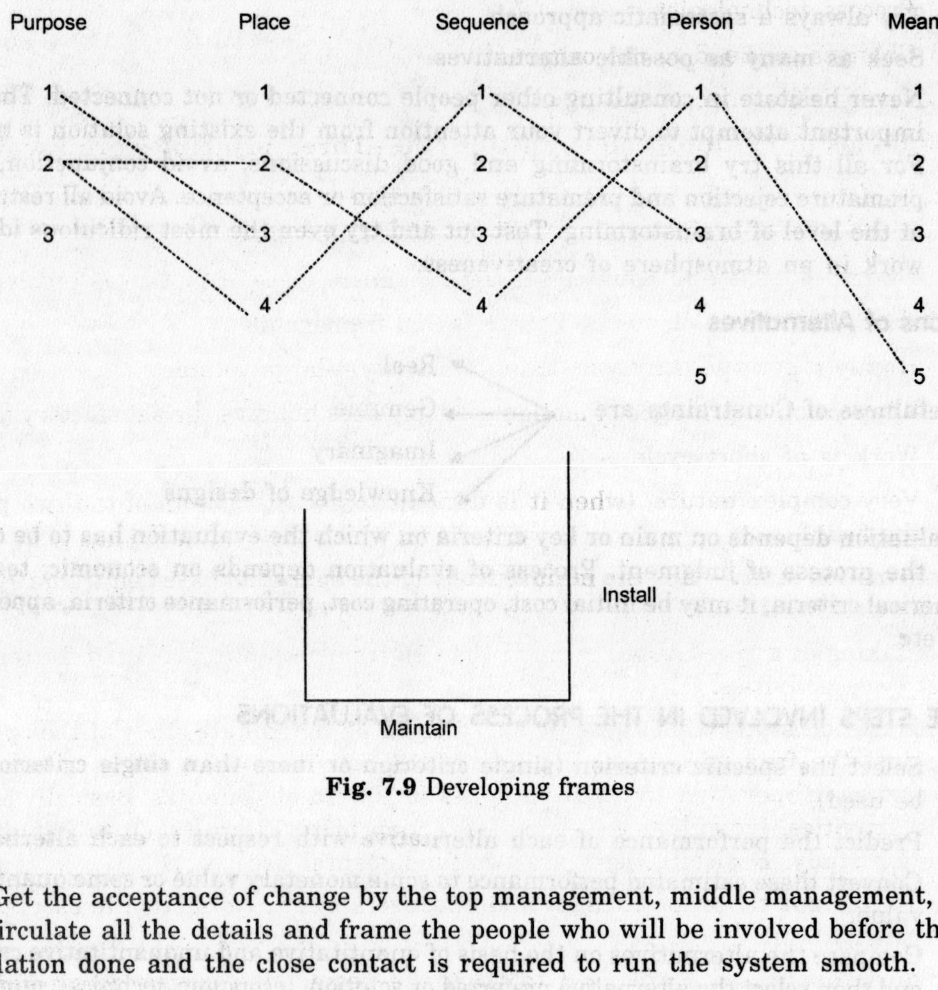

Fig. 7.9 Developing frames

Install

Get the acceptance of change by the top management, middle management, workers etc. Circulate all the details and frame the people who will be involved before the actual installation done and the close contact is required to run the system smooth.

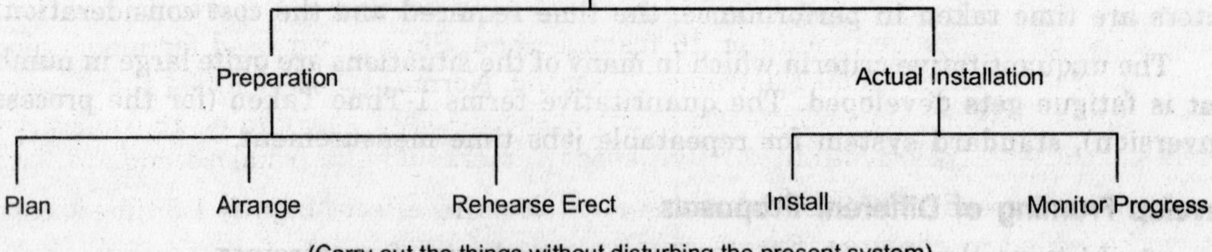

Fig. 7.10 Process of installation

7.11 PRINCIPLES OF MOTION OF ECONOMY

Motion Study (To the manual activity that movement of the parts of the body).

Class of change. Changes confined to

1. Human activities
2. Workplace layout tool and equipment
3. Process technologies
4. Changes confined to the output
5. Changes confined to the input.

Principles of motion economy (Gilbreth)—Three principles are involved.

1. In the use of human body (motion at macro level)
2. Arrangement of workplace (at the least possible time)
3. Design of tools and equipments used at micro class of motion is involved

At macro level basic elements Therbligs 960 frames/min

1. Highly repetitive activities (manual activity)—large volume
2. Application of principle of motion economy does not give the satisfactory analysis
3. Work is of short cycle
4. Very complex nature. (when it is difficult to get the motion of the two parts of the body).

Micro motion study—It is the minute study of the operation based on frame by frame analysis movie film/video.

Film taking at a speed equal or more than 16 frame/minute. It is used for repetitive and short cycle activities.

Memo motion study (time lapse) is also defined as the minute study of the operation based against the frame by frame analysis of the activities when taken in terms of a regular services in operation 15 frames/minutes to 100 frames/minutes. Basically used for long cycle activities, irregular cycle activity. Motion pictures are taken to complete the micro motion study. Basically there are two fundamental uses:

1. To find out the most efficient and effective sequence of motion to carry out the activity.
2. Basic applications are used to train the people, the correct method/effective method of performing the manual activity or sequence of operation.

Frame to Frame Analysis requires few frames to develop the shorter cycle. Normal speed cameras 960 frame/minute or 16 frame/second. Slow speed used for memo motion study cameras modified 15,60,120 frame/1/2 second. Normal speed modified that is normal speed /standard 1000 frame/minute. Commercial speed-1080 frame/minute 18 frame/second. Sound speed 1440 frames/minutes. High speed cameras 64-128 frame/second.

Very high speed 1000-3000 frames /second. Zooming effect-Magnify 1-5 time is carried out (to be added to camera). Frame counter is must.

7.12 WORK MEASUREMENT

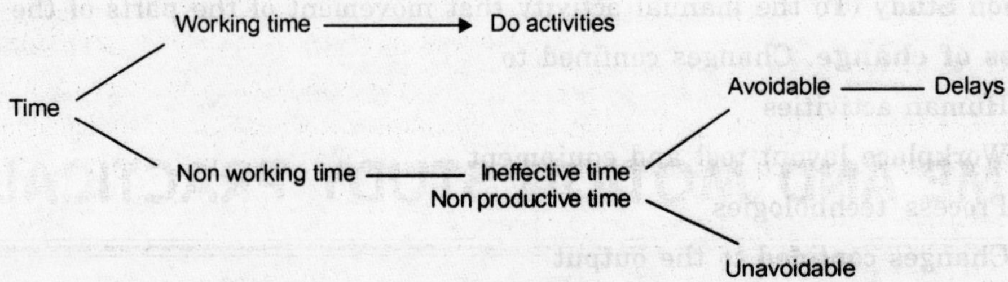

Fig. 7.11

Total time = Do time + Non productive time + Unavoidable delays.

Standard time work measurements in method study are used to compare the various alternatives : determining the schedule and plans of the organization and also used for estimating working cost, budgets, finding out the number of machines which could be assigned to one person, balancing the work of members of the team in group activities. They are used for making payment to the workers, incentive to both direct/indirect workers used for carrying out manpower planning, estimation of cost at the tender stage, estimation of selling price that is time taken in conversion of any given process.

Techniques of Work Measurement

1. Time study (stop watch study).
2. Production study (process study, activity study).
3. Work sampling (activity sampling, process sampling, ratio delay study).
4. Analytical estimation.
5. Synthetic standard data system (any can be divided into certain factors.
6. Predetermined motion time system (PMTS) applicable to manual activity.
7. Motion pictures.
8. Logging system (record the various activities and put the time and on an average find out the distribution of time into the various activities).
9. Determing the schedule and plans of the organization.
10. Estimating working cost and budgets.
11. Finding out the nos of m/es which could be asigned to one person.

8

CHAPTER

TIME AND MOTION STUDY PRACTICALS

8.1 TIME AND MOTION STUDY PRACTICALS

1-To study the existing method of Assembly of Bulb Holders with the layout as given and do the following.

Experiment

1. Prepare the Operation Process Chart.
2. Prepare the Two Handed Process Chart.
3. Draw the Learning Curve.
4. Determine the Cycle Time from the sufficient number of observations.
5. Develop the New Method and sequence of operation.
6. Prepare new Two Handed Process Chart.
7. Calculate the cycle time for the new method.

Table 8.1

L.H.S. L.H.S.

Date	Time	○	⇨	□	D	○	⇨	□	D

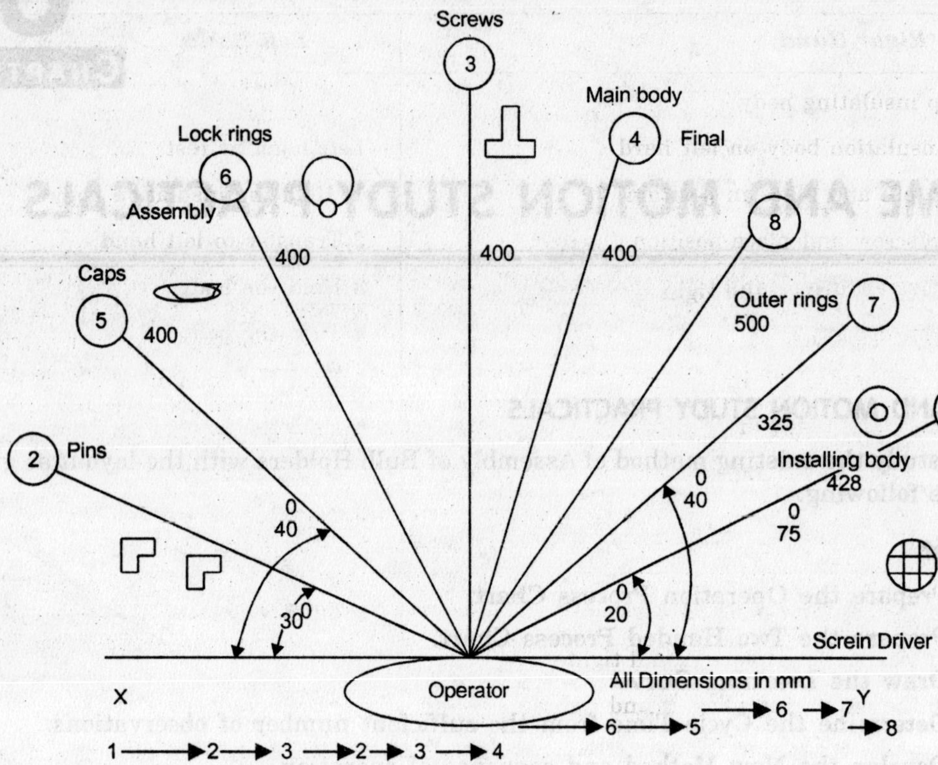
Screws
Main body
Final
Lock rings
Assembly
Caps
Outer rings
500
Pins
Installing body
428
325
400
400
400
400
40°
30°
40°
20°
75°
Screin Driver
Operator
All Dimensions in mm
X
Y
1 → 2 → 3 → 2 → 3 → 4
→ 6 → 5
→ 6 → 7
→ 8

Fig. 8.1

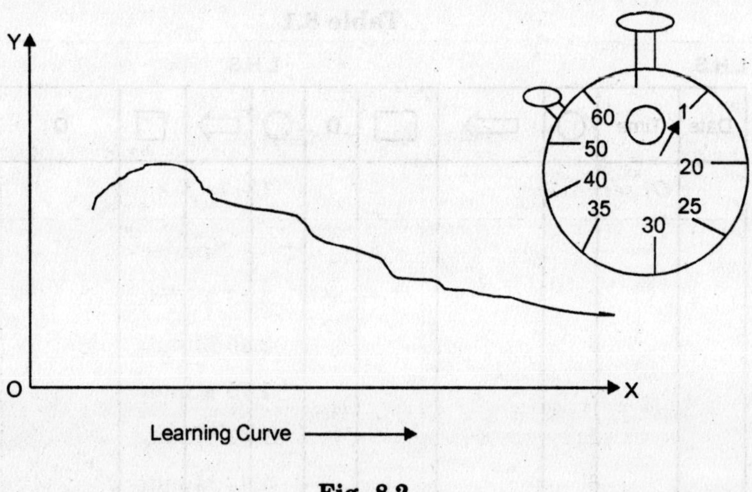
Y
O
X
Learning Curve
60
1
50
20
40
25
35
30

Fig. 8.2

Two Handed Process Chart

Right Hand	***Left Hand***
Pick up insulating body	
Place insulation body on left hard	Left hand at rest
Pick up pin and place in position	1. Hold the insulation body
Pick up screw and place position	2 Transfer to left hand
Pick up screw driver and tight the screw	3 Hold the body
The screw driver	4 Turn the body
Pick up pin and place in position	5 Hold the body
Pick screw and place in position	6 Hold the body
Pick up screw driver and tighten the screw	7 Hold the body
Pick up the main body	8 Turn body
Align the insulator	
Pick up the cap and place in position	9 Turn body
Pick up locking ring, place it and tighten	10 Hold
Pick up the outer ring place it and tighten	11 Turn the body
	12 Hold
Transport the body to assembly place	13 Turn the body
	14 Hold
	15 Hold

Table 8.2
First Oservation

Observation	***Cycle Time***
1	3 Minute
2	3.35 Minute
3	2.45 Minute
4	1.75 Minute
5	1.62 Minute
6	1.42 Minute
7	2.80 Minute
8	2.15 Minute
	Total 1854/8=2.317

Second Observation

Observation	*Cycle Time*
1	1–30
2	1–35
3	1–29
4	1–29
5	1–04
6	1–30
7	1–26
8	1–45
9	1–27
10	1–12
11	1–18

Third Observation

Observation	*Cycle Time*	*Observation*	*Cycle Time*	*Observation*	*Cycle Time*
1	1.30	12	1.28	23	1.52
2	1.35	13	1.30	24	1.10
3	1.25	14	1.28	25	1.23
4	1.20	15	1.35	26	1.43
5	1.22	16	1.35	27	1.27
6	1.18	17	1.40	28	1.40
7	1.20	18	1.32	29	1.4
8	1.22	19	1.60	30	1.3
9	1.25	20	1.42	31	1.28
10	1.28	21	1.50	32	1.25
11	1.30	22	1.48	33	1.27

Present Position

Found the problem with present work:

1. No cross movement.
2. Parts should be placed as per the easy picking up by the hands.
3. Change out the present system.
4. Change the layout.
5. Reduce the non productive method holding i.e., can be used on fixtures etc.
6. Several parts to be placed at point near to the place of operator.
7. Pre positioning of the parts.

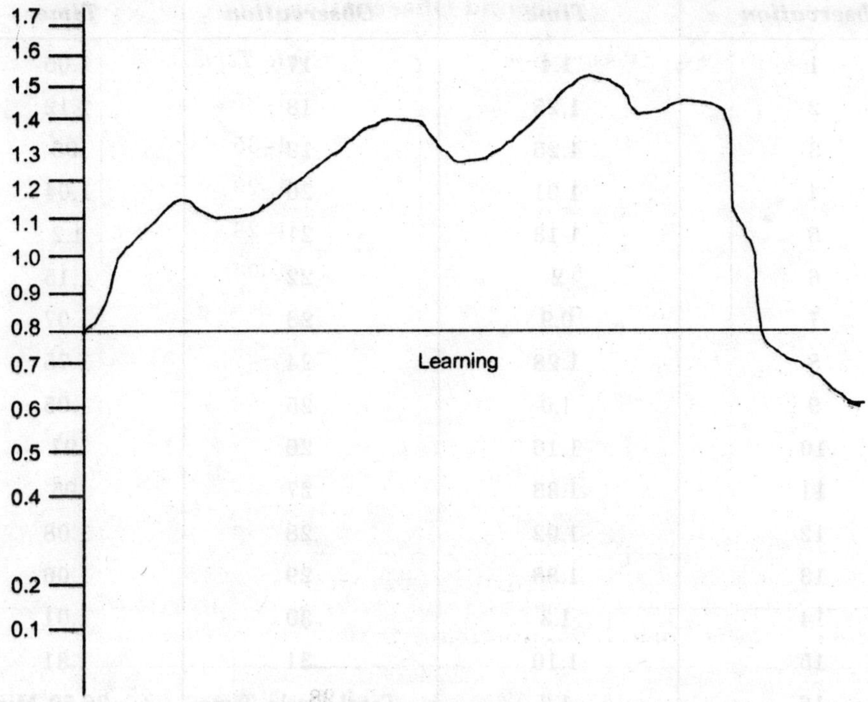

Fig. 8.3

New Layout

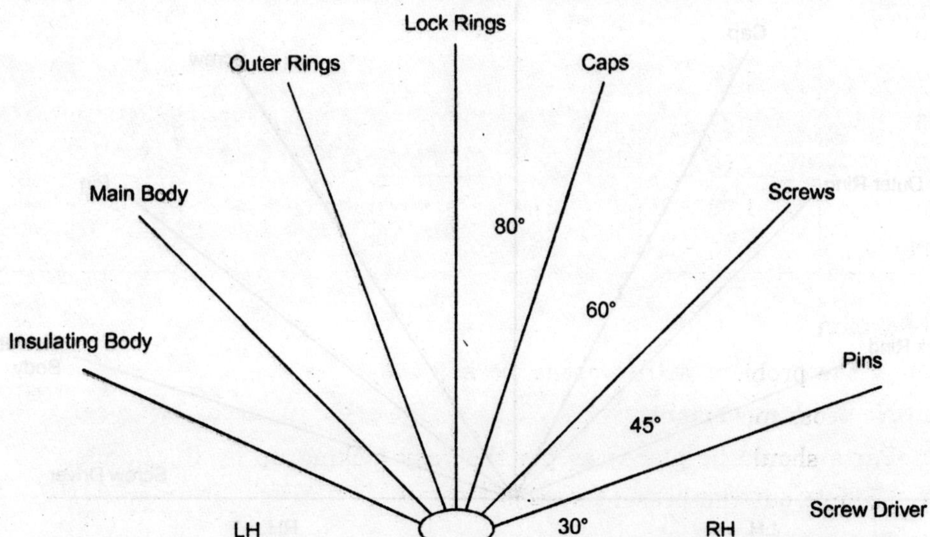

Fig. 8.4

Observation	*Time*	*Observation*	*Time*
1	1.4	17	1.05
2	1.25	18	1.12
3	1.25	19	.98
4	1.01	20	1.04
5	1.13	21	1.2
6	2	22	1.15
7	0.9	23	1.07
8	1.28	24	1.75
9	1.0	25	1.05
10	1.16	26	.97
11	1.35	27	.95
12	1.02	28	1.08
13	1.35	29	1.06
14	1.3	30	1.01
15	1.10	31	1.31
16	1.3	Total Cycle Time	36.59 Minute

New Layout

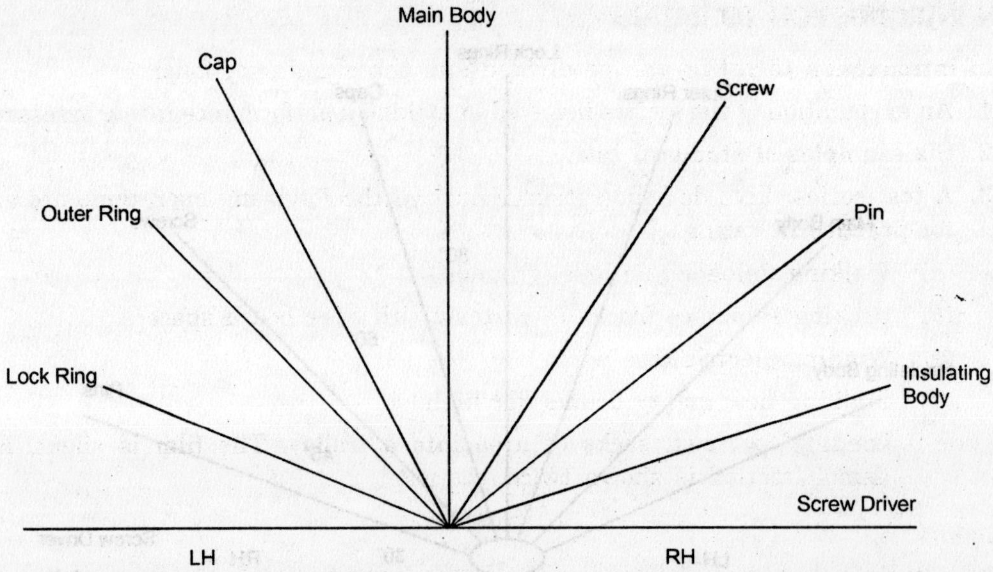

Fig. 8.5

Table 8.3

Observation	*Time*
1	0.81
2	1.01
3	.85
4	1.14
5	.92
6	1.09
7	1.06
8	0.91
9	0.85
10	0.82
Total Cycle Time	9.46 Minute

Card Distribution 52 card. Time taken 49 cent minutes normal time.

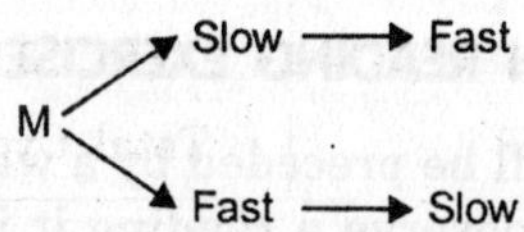

Walking 0.19 cent minutes for 50 meter distance.

8.2 AN INTRODUCTION TO RATING

An introduction to rating can be divided into three main sections:

1. An explanation of the factors involved in making a performance rating assessment.
2. Six examples of standard rating.
3. A test series: Five demonstration of each of the following operations are given for practice in rating.
   - (*a*) Walking unloaded on level ground.
   - (*b*) Packing salamace blocks in cartons with fiber board spacers.
   - (*c*) Winding electric fuse wire.
   - (*d*) Stalking new empty drums: for high.
   - (*e*) Loading 3×1 cwt, sacks of urea into a trolley. The film is silent. Each demonstration is shown twice.

Experiments

The film is designed to give some practice in rating for the beginner in time study. The experiment will be conducted in two parts.

1. Without feedback, 2. With feed back.

The audience will be given a record sheet for each of two parts:

1. *Without feed back*. In this experiment five different demonstrations of the same operation are shown twice with a slight gape. The first demonstration is for the sake of comprehensions while you have to rate after seeing it for the second times, when a time interval for recording the reading is given. In this method you don't get an instant feedback about the correctness of you estimate and you are liable to be biased towards either over rating or be in co-existence.
2. *With immediate feedback*. This part of the experiment is modified slightly to give you feed back on the error of your estimate in each of the demonstrations. This may lead to a quicker learning process as you will instantly know your tendency to over/under rate you may subsequently improve your rating. In this screening after seeing the demonstration first time you should record your rating in a slight time gape, while the demonstration is shown second time, the control rating will be announced by the instructor. Then during that time you can judge how much out of the estimate you are, which will sharpen your ability to rate subsequently. Analysis for both the parts arrange the reading in ascending order and plot them against the control rating reading.

Comment upon the trend (no trend you will get)

WATCH READING EXERCISE PART

Each showing of the watch will be preceded by a warning spot one second before each demonstration. Should you fall to observe a reading it is important that you indicate the omission with an-X

Table 8.4

Group A	**Group D**	33--------
1--------	16--------	34--------
2--------	17--------	35--------
3--------	18--------	36--------
4--------	**Group E**	37--------
5--------	21--------	38--------
Group B	22--------	39--------
6--------	23--------	**Group G**
7--------	24--------	41--------
8--------	25--------	42--------
Group C	**Group F**	43--------
9--------	26--------	44--------
10--------	27--------	45--------
11--------	28--------	**Group H**
12--------	29--------	46--------
13--------	30--------	47--------
14--------	31--------	48--------
15--------	32--------	49--------
		50--------

8.3 WORK MEASUREMENT PROJECT (RATING ACTUAL WALKING)

Equipment and Materials Needed. Decimal minute stop watch, steel tape, chalk string, Rating Form.

Place-Select a room with smooth level floor or use a smooth level side-wal.

Procedure for conducting Rating Study:

1. Measure off 50 feet of unobstructed floor space, marking a starting and a stopping line on the floor and allowing 10 to 15 feet of additional space at either end for the operator to start and stop. Tie a string to the back of one chair and throw it across the back of another chair so that the string is stretched directly above the starting line on the floor. Also place a string across two chairs at the other end of the 50 feet. These strings are to be better enable the operator to start his watch and read his watch at the proper instant.
2. Have someone (this person will be called the operator) practice walking the 50 feet at exactly three miles per hour. This practice should take place before the group assembles. The operator should take 189 minute to walk the 50 feet. After a little practice it will not be difficult for the operator to walk the 50 feet in this time or at a speed of 3 miles per hour table -1 shows the time needed for the operator to walk 50 feet at other speeds.
3. Provide each person with a data sheet and rating graph for walking can be prepared.
4. The operator then walks the 50 feet ten different times called trial he records on his data sheet the actual time it took him to walk the 50 feet and the corresponding rating in percent. The walking speed should fall between approximately 2.50 miles per hour 85% of normal and 4.5 % miles per hour 150% of normal.
5. Each person watches the operator walk the 50 feet and rates him using 100%=3 miles per hour as normal.

Performance and Rating

It is the mental comparison by the work study man of the performance of the operator under observation will be own idea of standard performance for a given value.

1. The rating must not be influenced imposed by the nature of work. Rating should be for a minimum acceptable quality standard. Short cycle should be rated whole cycle wise. Longer cycle should be rated element wise. Accuracy of the rating is (+–) 5%.

8.4 FACTORS EFFECTING THE RATING

1. Effectiveness a—Skill of the operator, b---Efficiency of the physical facilities and tools and equipments.
2. Effort
3. Speed

Effectiveness depends on the physical facilities.

Various methods of estimating performance rating (observation method only and depends on the skill of the worker)

1. **Speed or Tempo Rating Method (Level of the motion of the motor parts of the body *i.e.*, output level).**
2. **Skill and effort rating method (Effectiveness and efforts) Charles Bedause method) *i.e.*, Normalization.**
3. **Westing out System of Performance Rating.**
4. **Synthesis Rating Method.**
5. **Objective Rating Method.**
6. **Physiocological Evaluation Performance Rating Method.**

Assembly Line (Comparing Various Persons)

- Skill
- Effort—subdivided into—Super Skill------A1,A2 +.15,.13

  Excellent------B1 B2 +.11,.08

  Good------C1,C2 +.06,.03

  Average------D----0

  Fair--------E1 E2-- - .05,-.10

  Poor------F1 F2--- -.16, -.22
- Working Condition
- Consistency

  Objective

Excessive	Excellent	Good	Average	Fair	Poor
A1 A2	B1 B2	C1 C2	D	E1 E2	F1 F2
+.13 .12	.10 .08	.05 .02	0	-.04 -.08	-.12 -.17

Working Condition

Ideal	Excellent	Good	Average	Fair	Poor
A	B	C	D	E	F
+.06	.04	.02	0	-.03	-.07

Consistency

Perfect	Excellent	Good	Average	Fair	Poor
A	B	C	D	E	F
+.04	+.03	.01	0	-.02	-.04

Changing in the operating system, variations are not in the control of the workers.

Interest, Aptitude, Level of skill effects the efficiency of worker.

Synthetic Rating Method-Basically based on the performance rating *i.e.*, Manual work (PMTS) *i.e.*, synthesis time (Therbligs and motion involved)

Normal Time = OT × PR

(Observed Time) × Performance Rating

Divide work into various elements:

Table 8.5

Synthetic	***OT(Time) By time study***	***Synthetic time (OT X PR) (By Any PMTS Method)***	***Ratio of Synthetic Time / PR (OT)*** ***B/A***
E1	.08	.09	1.125
E2	.09	.095	1.056
E3	1.00	1.20	1.200
E4	1.20	1.44	1.200
E5	4.25	4.00	.941
E6	5.02	4.50	.896
E7	.15	-----	-----
E8	.23	-----	-----
AVG	1.502		6.418/6 = 1.0697

8.5. OBJECTIVE RATING METHOD

Two tier performance level at first measured in first method at second step correction factor job difficulties table values.

1. **Amount of the body used.**
2. **Foot Pedals.**
3. **Use of two arms.**
4. **Eye hand coordination.**
5. **Handling requirements.**
6. **Weight of the body used like (Motor parts of the body)**

$$PR = PR_1 (1+S)$$

(Actual Performance Rating)

S-Correction factor (Get the value from table)

PR1-Performance rating in first method.

Physiological Evaluation Method-

Human Energy (Biological process or Metabolic process)

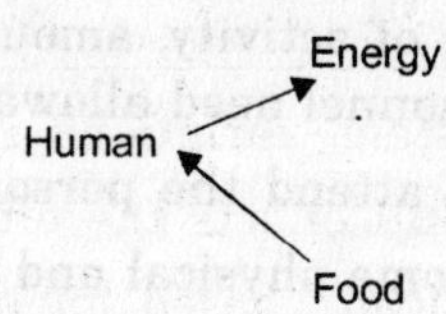

4100-4800 Kcal produces energy out of this 40-50% is used *i.e.*,

2000 ⟶ 100Kcal

8.6. TIME STUDY ALLOWANCES

(The period when no work is done *i.e.*, used for some other work etc.

U.I.T. U ⟶ Unavoidable

I ⟶ Inefficient

T ⟶ Time

Standard Time ⟶ NT + Ineffective Time

(Normal time)+Allowance % of NT or ST

ST = NT + A

Normal Time+ Allowance

= NT+A% of NT

= NT (1+A)

ST-A of ST = NT

ST(1-A) = NT

ST = NT/1-A

Ineffective Time-Complete analysis to be done which are not unavoidable.

Allowances may of these types-

1. **Physical fatigue or rest.**
2. **For Tea.**
3. **For Personnel need.**
4. **Shortage of Materials etc.**

Due to make ready and preparation put away activity ineffective time.

8.7. TYPE OF ALLOWANCES

1. Process Allowance (Unavoidable delay allowances).
2. Relaxation-Rest or fatigue allowance, Personnel allowance.
3. Special Allowances-Periodic activity allowance, Interference allowance.
4. Policy allowance.

Out of 04 allowances 2 and 3 are time study allowance to be compensated and 1 if piece rate or incentive system (due to this part of time study) and 4 is the policy allowance *i.e.*, management policy.

Relaxation Time. Relaxation time with addition to the normal time to the worker. This amt depends upon the nature of activity, amount of attention required, motivation factors, fatigue allowances and personnel need allowance, human body working condition.

Personnel allowance-Given to attend the personnel need.

Fatigue allowance. To overcome physical and mental fatigue. The physical fatigue are of two types-cost allowance and other is variable allowance (cost allowances are those allowances which are basically take care of basic matriculsium (*i.e.*, even if the work is not performed you have to give allowance). Nature of the activity and where the man is involved to estimate the various allowances and these factors are involvement of human body while working, use of muscular energy or force, various working conditions, light, noise, atmospheric conditions mental strain, physical strain, job satisfaction, tediousness incentives etc.

Special allowances. All those which are not part of the activity but they do occur in regular or irregular activity (time spent or make ready activity *i.e.*, at regular interval) Power failure at regular interval or power failure at irregular intervals.

Interference allowance. Cause to the two activity going at one time for example machine work.

Contingency allowance. Under this there are certain activity which may occur due to some reason for example strike etc. (time which cannot be estimated *i.e.*, they do waist time.)

Policy allowance. A special creation at special condition *i.e.*, under the discretion of the management.

8.8 METHODS OF WORK MEASUREMENT

Production study/Process study/Activity study. Estimation of the ineffective time-Estimation of the allowance finding out the accuracy.

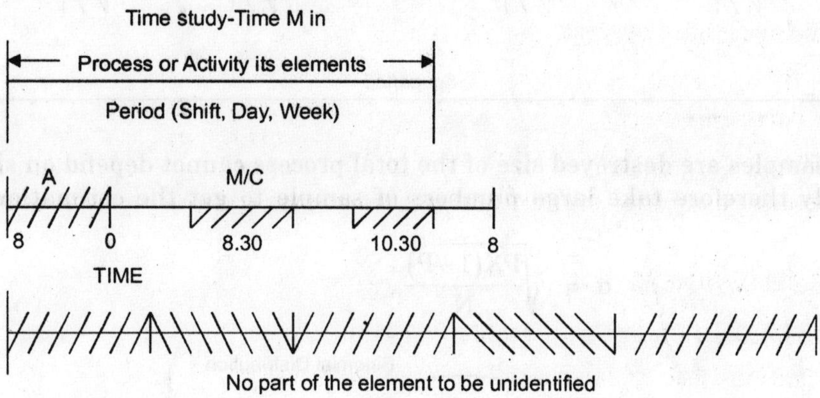

8.9 PRODUCTION STUDY

It is a study carried out over a specified period of time for the purpose of ascertaining the frequency and duration of activity like effective time, infrequent occurrence of activities and various other activities. Production study can be used for various uses.

1. To find the % of in effective time.
2. To find the occurrence of special allowances (contingency allowance)
3. To find the % performance of utilization of the machine or activity.
4. To find the % of different people or different activity.
5. To find the record of the perfectness of the departments.

The accuracy of the time standard set by time study to be used for finding out the output of each individuals and their trends. Production study is always carried out in series over a specified period after a gap of certain specified time (2 days and then gap and then after one week like this over a specified period to find out the accurate result at the end. Stop watch or ordinary watch used for measurement of time.

8.10 WORK SAMPLING

(Activity Sampling/Ratio Delay study *i.e.*, non occurrence of activity).

Sampling process on the basis of statistics we assume that whatever true to the sample. For cooking of rice in a container you can take one part of rice that will give the sample.

8.11. BASIC LAW OF PROBABILITY

Four basic aspect for sample:

1. Random sample or sample must be taken instantaneously.
2. Intermittent
3. Unbiased
4. Instantanously

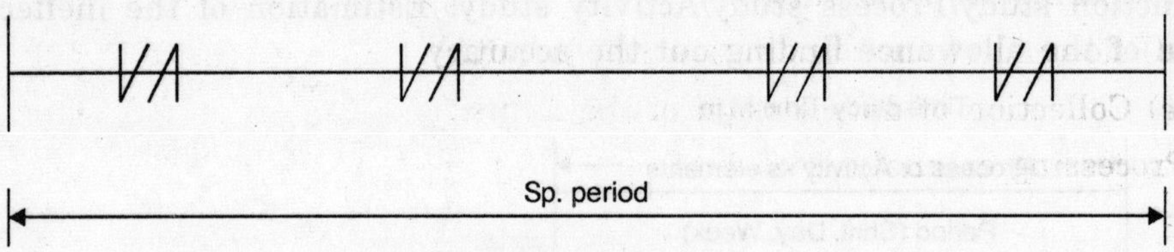

When samples are destroyed size of the total process cannot depend on single sample in time study therefore take large numbers of sample to get the estimation.

$$\sigma = \sqrt{\frac{PX(1-P)}{N}}$$

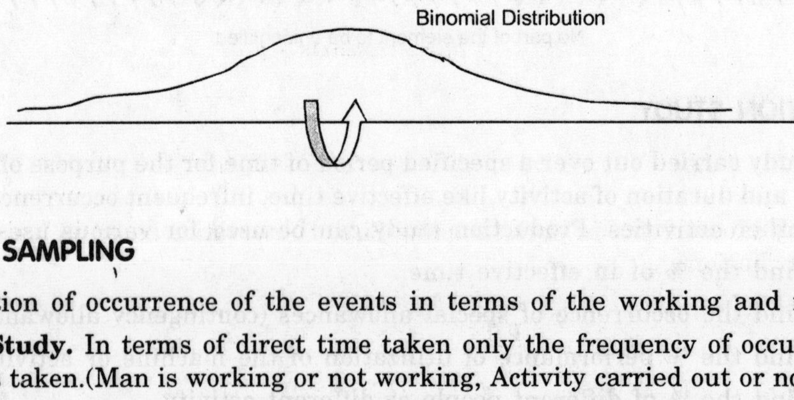

8.12 WORK SAMPLING

Proportion of occurrence of the events in terms of the working and not working.

Time Study. In terms of direct time taken only the frequency of occurrence or non occurrence is taken.(Man is working or not working, Activity carried out or not carried out)

	Activity	
	ON	OFF
Find of both	%	%

Probability of both occurring is 1, p (Non occurrence of activity) and (1– p) = q

P = Number of frequencies (to be observed) to the non occurrence of activity.

Q = Occurrence of activity

$$P = \frac{\text{No of Frequency Non occurrence}}{\text{No of total frequency Non occurrence}}$$

Work sampling involves the estimation of proportion of the time devoted to the given activity or a part of activity over a certain specified period of time by means of taking sufficient no of observations which are random. Intermittent, Instantaneous and unbiased. The basis of sampling is the law of probability.

Work Sampling. Process of Work Study

1. Define the total activity/process.
2. Define the sampling process.
   (*a*) The total specified period of time.
   (*b*) Number of observations to be made.
   (*c*) Timings of observation.
   (*d*) Routing of the observation *i.e.*, layout.
   (*e*) Collection of data /design of the forms.
3. Processing or analysis of data.

8.13 WORK SAMPLING (RATIO DELAY)

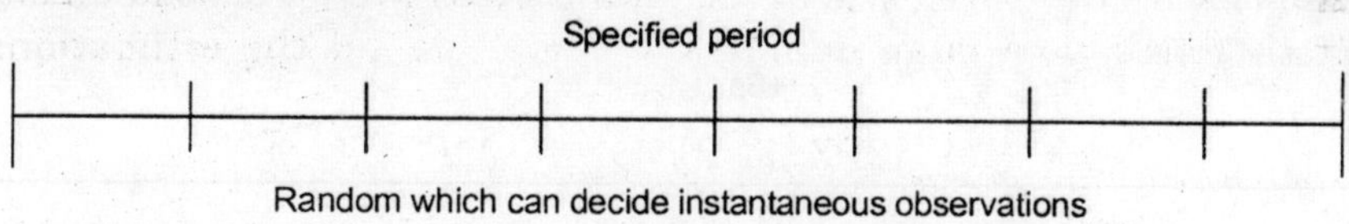

Initial Sample 100 observation for carrying out the activity.

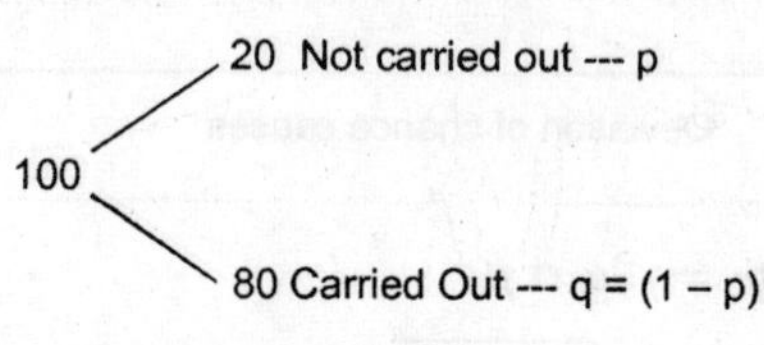

Probability of occurrence in work sampling-Size of observation based on law of probability (Binomial Distribution)

$$\text{S.D.} = \sqrt{\frac{p.q}{N}}$$

$$\text{S.D.} = \sqrt{\frac{p(1-p)}{N}}$$

Large number of observation Binomial distribution → Normal Distribution

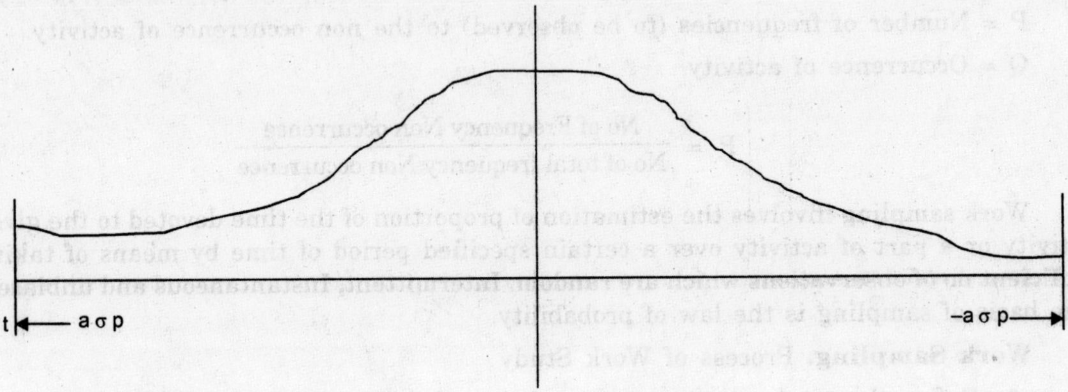

a = **Coefficient of confidence interval**

s-**Accuracy**

I-Interval

$$\sigma = \sqrt{\frac{p(1-p)}{N}}$$

$$a = 3$$

$$a = 2$$

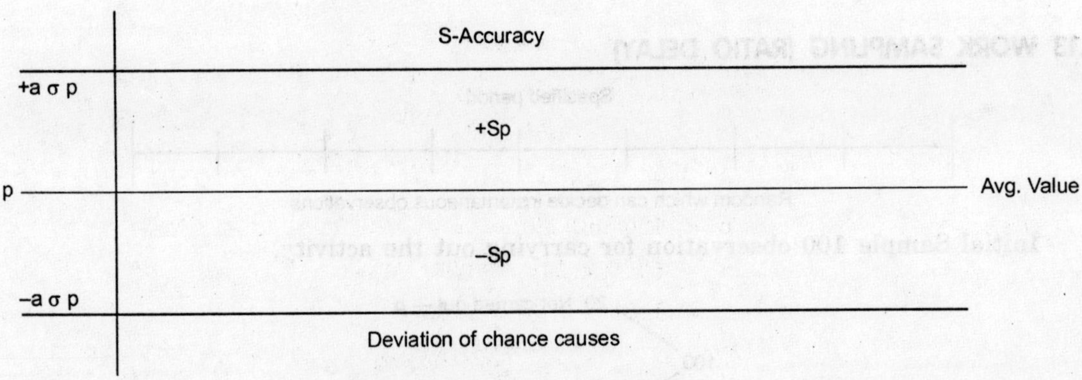

$$2sp = 2a\,\sigma\,p$$

$$= a\sqrt{\frac{p(1-p)}{N}}$$

$$+\ s^2p^2 = \frac{a^2 p(1-p)}{N}$$

$$N = \frac{a^2 p(1-p)}{s^2\, p^2}$$

$$\left(\frac{a}{s}\right)^2 \cdot \frac{(1-p)}{p}$$

$p = 0 \quad N = \infty$

$p = 1 \quad N = 0$

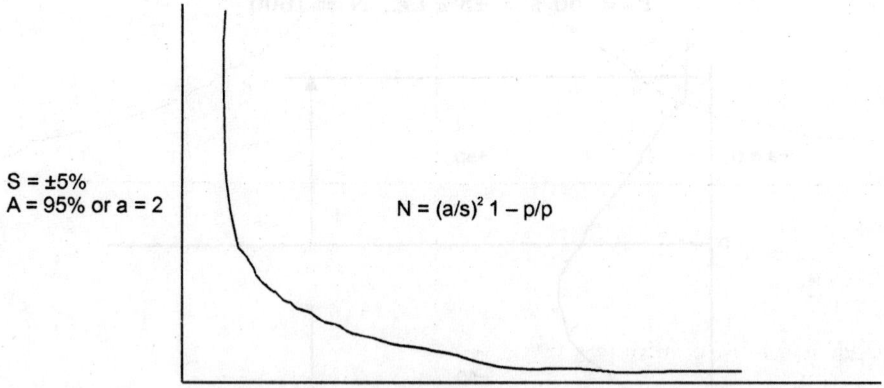

$N = (2/.05)^2\ 1-p/p$

$.20 \longrightarrow 100$

$N = 1600.1-p/p = 64$

Take 600 observation find p = .35

N = 595 if N is just equal to 600 then stop.

If taken 500 observation → 350–working, → 150–Non Working

i.e., $p = 150/350 = .30$

$N = 1600 \times 1 - .30/.30$

$= 1600 \times .7/.3 = 3733$

If 4000 observation → 2600-Working, → 1400-Non-Working

Find out they are sufficient or not and a taken as 2

$P = 1400/4000 = .35$

$$Sp = 2\sqrt{\frac{p(1-p)}{N}}$$

$$S \times .35 = 2\sqrt{\frac{0.35 \times 65}{4000}} = \pm 4.3\% \textit{ i.e., } 5\% \text{ sufficient}$$

Absolute Error of Mean:

Let us say $p = 1$ s = ±5% $a = 2$ p = small take large numbers of observation *i.e.*, N = 158400

$$P = 50 \quad s = \pm 5\% \quad i.e., \; N = 1600$$

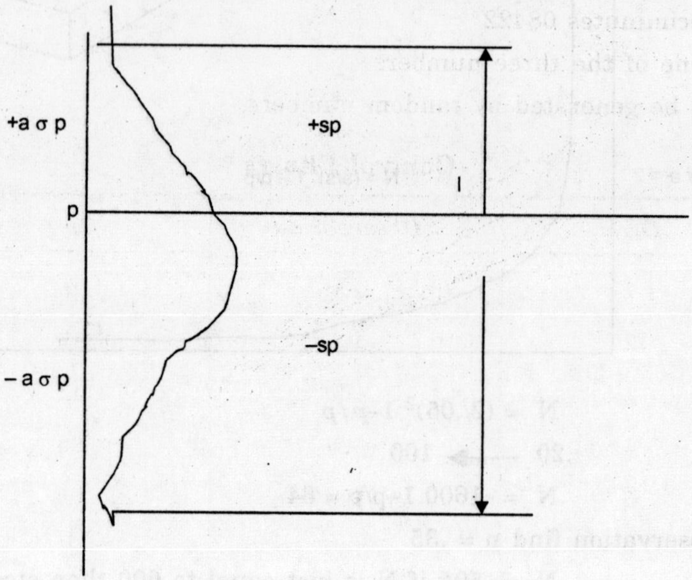

$$I = 2sp$$

$I = 2a\,p$ (take this two values since they are superimposed.)

$$I = I_1$$

$$= 2a\,\sigma\,p$$

$$I = 2a\sqrt{\frac{p(1-p)}{N}}$$

$$I^2 = \frac{4a^2\,p(1-p)}{N}$$

i.e., $N = 4(a/I)\,p(1-p)$

$$P = 0 \quad N = 0$$

$$P = 1 \quad N = 0$$

$$N = 4\left(\frac{a}{I}\right)^2 p(1-p)$$

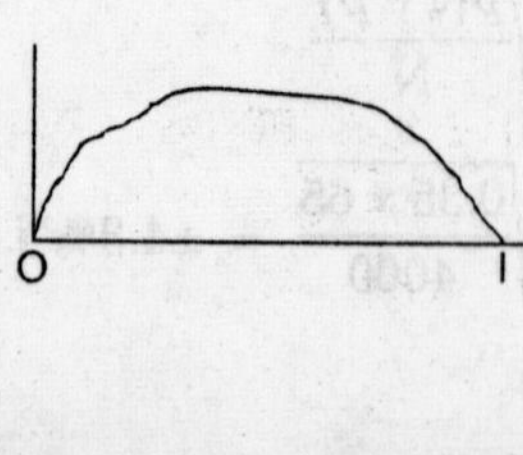

Randomness can be used by means of generating the random timings at which the observation should be taken. Generate by dies random number tables.

1 hrs & 0 deciminute 10097

3 hrs 75 deciminutes 37542

0 hrs 84 deciminutes 08422

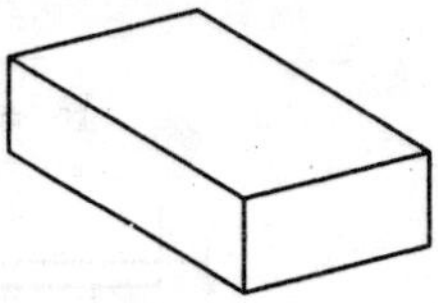

Take any one of the three numbers.

Timings can be generated by random numbers.

Control Charts

Days	*Observation*	*p*
1	100	9
2	100	10
3	100	12
4	100	08
5	100	06
6	100	20
7	100	23
8	100	18
9	100	16
10	100	10
11	100	15
12	100	09
13	100	08
14	100	06

$$\overline{p} = \frac{p_1 + p_2 + p_3 + ...n}{100}$$

Control Chart Limits = $\overline{p} \pm 3$ sigma

$$= \overline{p} \pm 3\sqrt{\frac{p(1-p)}{n}}$$

$$= .10 \pm 3 \times .03$$

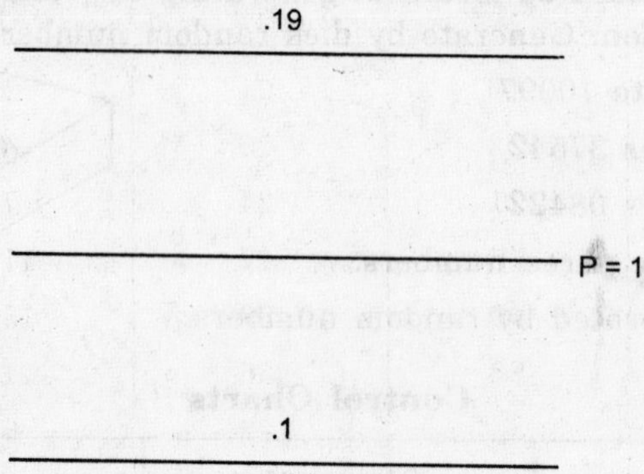

8.14 WORK STUDY FOR ESTABLISHING THE STANDARD TIME FOR A GIVEN ACTIVITY

Total output, total working time, involvement of the man power. Let us consider some activity is going on there are 10 workers involved giving to the same output which is measurable in terms of number of units for a given time we would like to get the standard time specifying a period let 3 days that is end of 3 days the total output can be found out. Total working time of 10 workers. Find out the ratio of the ideal time and the total working time. Average PR of workers.

$$\text{Standard Time ST} = \frac{\text{Total working time in minutes} \times \%\text{ weight} \times \text{Avg. PR}}{\text{Total Output}} + \text{Allowances}$$

If time is not available

Total time in minutes

Workers	×	hrs	×	days	×	minutes
10	×	8	×	3	×	60

% wt can be found from work sampling

Example. 10 workers are working to produce the same type of parts.

Total time spent in 3 days 13650 minute

$$= 10 \times 3 \times 8 \times 60 = 1400$$

Total Allowance = 15% of ST

Total output in 3 days = 16314 pieces

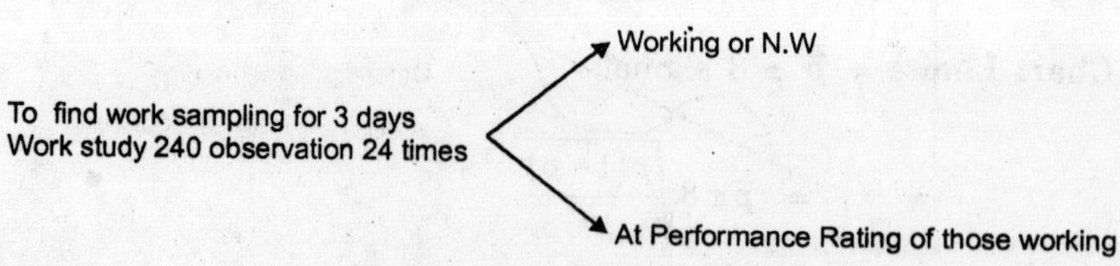

PR	1st	2nd	3rd	AVG	WT AVG × PR
100	03	06	01	10	1000
105	13	22	09	44	4620
110	32	21	24	77	8470
115	48	45	17	110	12650
120	47	49	39	135	16200
125	27	28	56	111	13675
130	26	30	22	61	7970
135	15	08	11	34	4590
140	14	15	22	51	7140
145	08	20	27	55	7975
150	02	10	11	23	3459
	235	237	239	711	84900

240 observations/day 24 times 3 day 240 × 3 = 720

84900/711 = 123.6% and 711/720 = .987

$$ST = \frac{13650 \times .987 \times 1.236}{16314} \times \frac{100}{85} = 120\,\text{MIN}$$

Analytical Estimation-Past Experience.

8.15. SYNTHESIS FROM STANDARD

(Developing one relationship may be in the form of equations). The contents involving carry out the activity. Time taken for the activity is based on the involvement of certain number of variables and their characteristics and their behavior. Variable *i.e.,* in certain trends for example to make shirt time depends on type of cloth, size, major or minor variables. The major variables takes 90-95% of time and minor variables takes 2-5% of time.

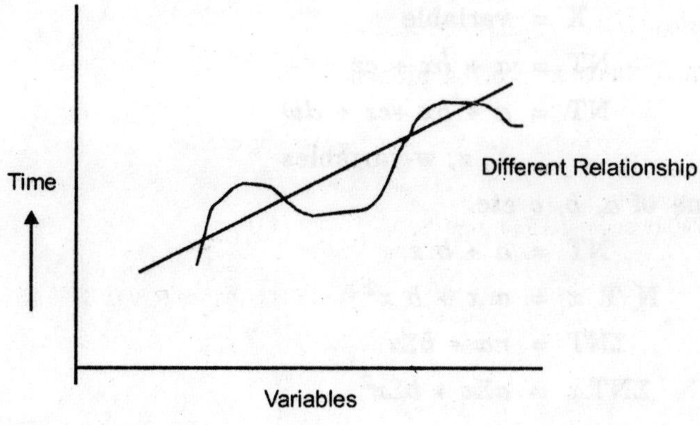

$$NT \propto f(V1, V2, V3 \text{---------------} Vn)$$

NT = a1v1-bv2-cv3-dv4 a1 = based on their behavioral aspects

2 3 4

Av1 + bv2 -cv3

$$NT = 1.56 + 3.5\,V1 - 4.5V2 + 0.45\,V3$$

$$NT \propto f(v1, v2, v3 \text{------------} vn)$$

$$NT = f(v1 + v2 + v3 + v4 + \text{------} vn)$$

$$NT = f(v1) + f(v2) + f(v3) + \text{-----} f(vn)$$

$$NT = NTE1 + NTE2 + NTE3 \text{-------------} NTEn$$

E1 = Elements

$$NTE1 = f(v1 + v2)$$

$$NTE2 = f(v1 + v2 + v3)$$

$$NTE3 = f(R1 + R2 + R3 + R4)$$

Important technique used is linear regression technique.

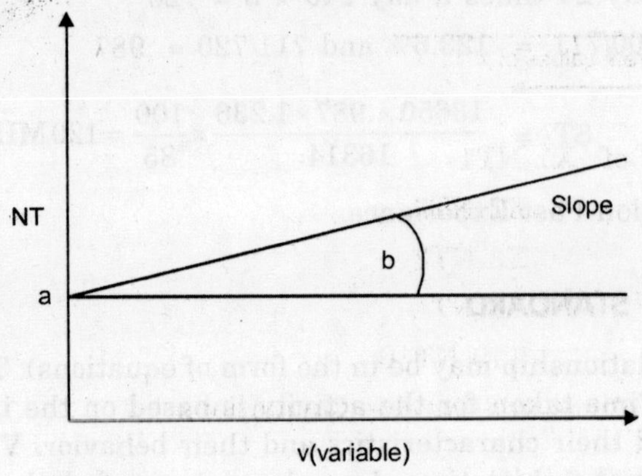

$$NT = a + bx$$

A = coefficient

X = variable

$$NT = a + bx + cz$$

$$NT = a + bx + cz + dw$$

X, z, w-variables

To get the value of *a, b, c* etc.

$$NT = a + b\,x$$

$$N\,T.\,x = a\,x + b\,x^2$$

$$\Sigma NT = na + b\Sigma x \qquad \text{...(1)}$$

$$\Sigma NT.x = a\Sigma x + b\Sigma x^2 \qquad \text{...(2)}$$

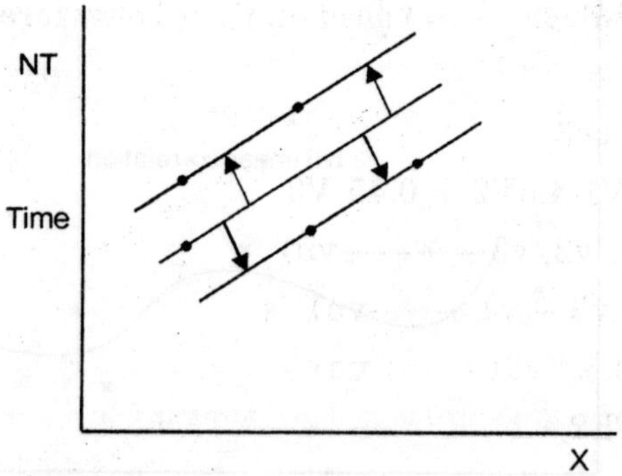

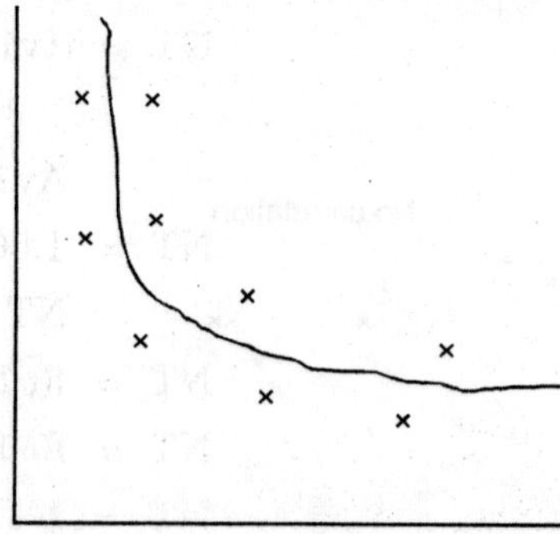

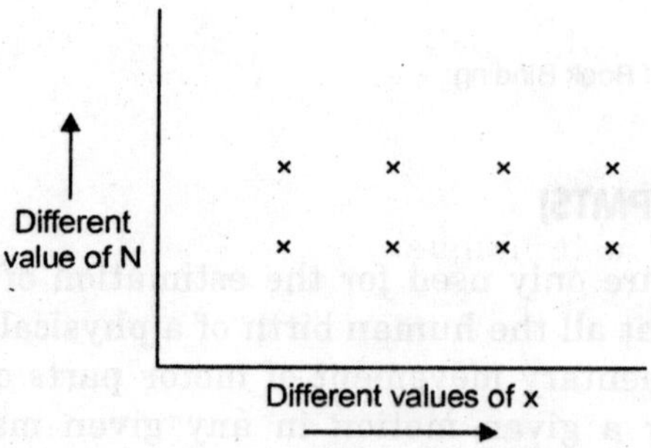

For a given value of X1 NT1

X2 NT2

X3 NT3

X4 NT4

X10 NT10

Take 10-20 observations and develop 2 equations

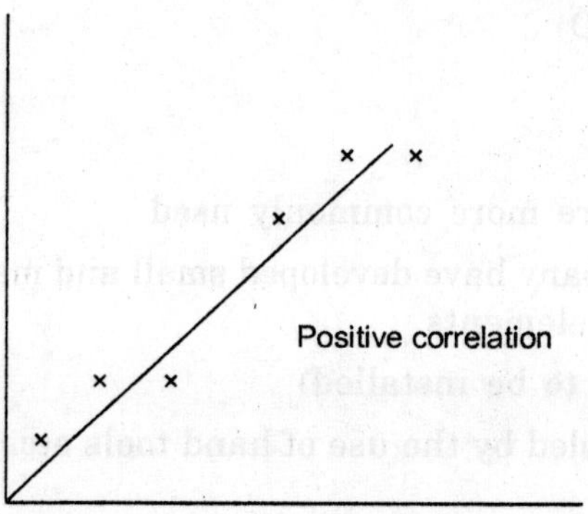

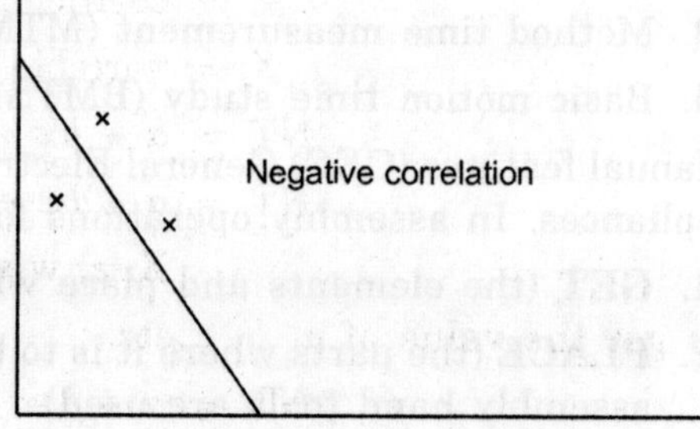

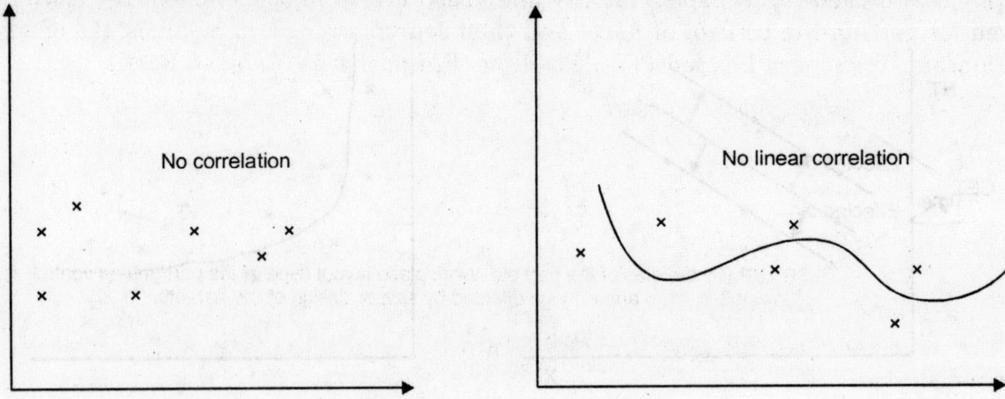

Examle-Printing Press of Book Binding

8.16. PRE DETERMINED MOTION TIME SYSTEM (PMTS)

Special form of standard data used which are only used for the estimation of time of manual activity. The basic concept of PMTS that all the human birth of a physical kind consists of different combination of basic or elementary movement of motor parts of the body. A PMTS is the expected performance for a given motion in any given manual operation or an activity which has been obtained by average the performance time of large no of persons in the performance of that basic motion."

A PMTS is a set of these pre-determined motion times from which it is possible to synthesis the performance time of a large nos of manual operations. Sum of these pre-determined motion times for a given activity gives the estimation of the normal time of the activity ST.

Advantages (Initially planning, organization and pre estimation of time) directs the NT *i.e.*, total working time, selection of method. Little accuracy simplified PMTS tables are available based on

1. Motion time data for assembly work (MTD)
2. Work factor system (WFS)
3. Method time measurement (MTM)
4. Basic motion time study (BMTS) b & c are more commonly used

Manual features (GEC) General Electrical Company have developed small and medium size appliances. In assembly operations four basic elements.

1. **GET** (the elements and place where it is to be installed)
2. **PLACE** (the parts where it is to be assembled by the use of hand tools etc. doing assembly hand tools are used)
3. **USE**
4. **DISPOSED OFF** (once the assembly is done after doing the work the part to be disassembled.

System recognizes two elements GET & PLACE is effected by size weight and type of the part but also effected by set of the work place, how the parts have been placed and basic physical elements, transport facility and grasp are two basic elementary motion are involved for getting the control of parts and then search and select involves use of search operation etc. Transport Loaded (TL), Position (Pre-position), Release Load)

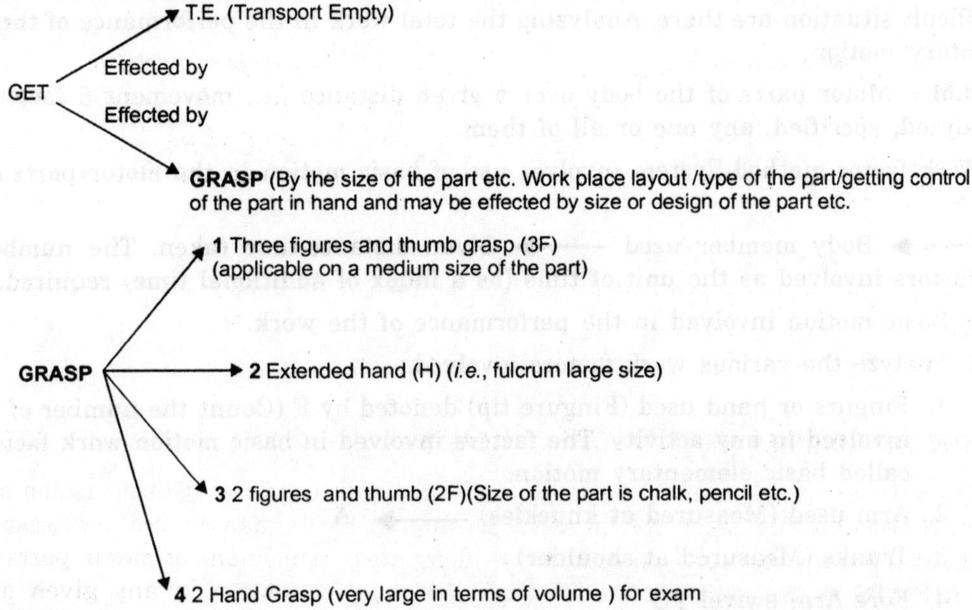

8.17 CONDITIONS OF GRASP HOW THEY EFFECT THE VARIABLE *i.e.,* TIME

Class A. Very best condition is available for example work station pre-positioning the work and grasp is not hindered by other objects most of the time search and select is missing *i.e.,* easily get the control of the parts.

Class B. Good grasping facility here parts to an large quantity requires sometimes search and select and the part may not be using any amount of force.

Class C. Not very good grasping facility the design of the part prevents ready grasp. Parts may be tangled with each other and may have to separate out the parts.

8.18 PLACE

Basically requires the fixturing of the parts/placing of the parts and consists of three based on the amount of the force needed the part has to be placed there. The condition of the place into four types.

(*a*) Example picking up duster and placing on table. Predetermined or undetermined position. No force required to place the parts moving the object from grasp (control).

(*b*) Positioning of the parts on/into a define location will amper tolerance something like simple fixture, assembly of part to another part, visual attention is required. No force is required.

(*c*) Positioning is difficult on complicated location closer exact tolerance with respect to the definite locations. Need a some short of force to place, release the part there.

(*d*) Same as in condition C and involves lot of care to handle while handling the parts. Small force is needed to fix the part or tightening the part.

8.19 WORK FACTOR SYSTEM

It is defined as a index of additional time required over and above the basic time needed in the performance of the given activity. It takes care of the condition under which the difficult situation are there. Analyzing the total work in the performance of the basic elementary motion.

B.M = Motor parts of the body over a given distance *i.e.*, movement 5 factors can be analyzed, specified, any one or all of them.

Work factor method-System involves use of basic motion in the motor parts of the body.

⟶ Body member used ⟶ Given distance/time taken. The numbers of work factors involved as the unit of time (as a index of additional time) required.

1. Basic motion involved in the performance of the work.
2. Analyze the various work factors involved.
   1. Fingurs or hand used (Fingure tip) denoted by F (Count the number of factor involved in any activity. The factors involved in basic motion work factor are called basic elementary motion.
   2. Arm used (Measured at knuckles) ⟶ A
   3. Trunks (Measured at shoulder)
   4. Fore Arm swivel FS
   5. Foot (Measured at Toe) FT
   6. Leg (Measured at Ankle) L
   7. Head Turn (Measured at Neck)NT

Body Member	Distance Moved	Weight	No of Factor
A	250	10Kg	SD
F	50	D	
F	25		

Utilities—

1. Transport (Reach & Move) TRT
2. Grasp GP
3. Preposition PP
4. Assemble ASY
5. Use (Manual process m/c time Use
6. Disengage DSV
7. Mental process MP
8. Release RL

Four major variables

1. Body member used.
2. Distance moved.

3. Work factor involved.
4. Weight carried or resistance overcome.

4 WF (Manual control)

1. Direction control WF (Steering)---S
2. Care (Precautions)--P
3. Change in direction--U (Angular Movement)
4. Definite stop--D

Example-Analyze the motion required

Perform activity and come back to the original position

1. TE (Reach) to the pen holder
   A 300 D .0065
   (Arm) (Distance)
2. Grasp the pen ½ F 25 S.0008 Unit
3. Move the pen A 300d .0065 units

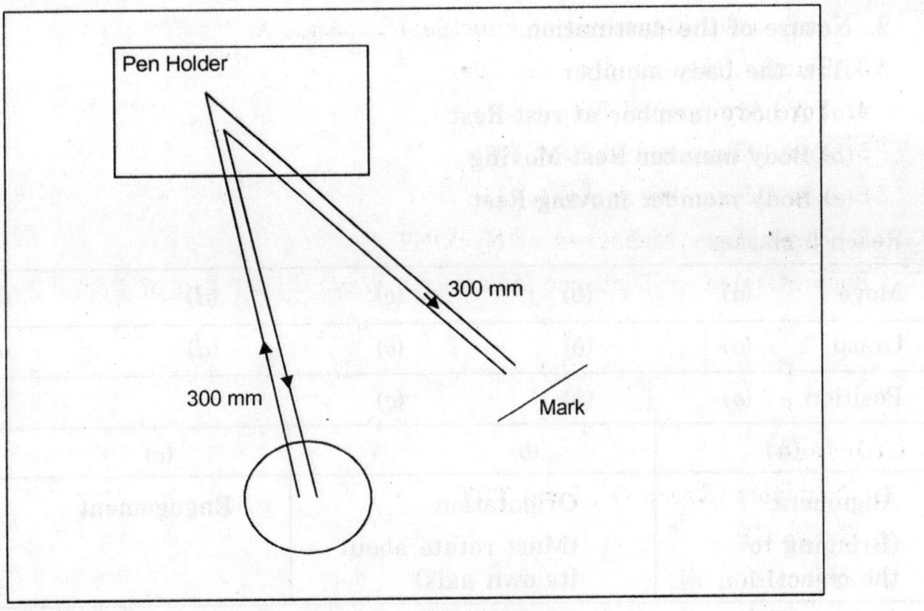

4. Position the pen at the paper F 25 SD .0029
5. Mark 1st stroke × F25SD .0023 units
6. Position pen on paper again F 25 SD .0029
7. Move the pen to the holder A 300D 65
8. Align pen to the M ¼ F 25 SP .007
9. Insert the pen to the holder F25 P .0023
10. Release the pen ½ F25 .003
11. Move at back A 300D .0061

8.20 METHOD TIME MEASUREMENT SYSTEM (MTM)

This is a procedure which analyze any mental work into basic motion required to perform the work which is determined by the nature of the motion and the condition under which this basic motion is performed. It is a motion which involves least amount of difficulty or precision for any given distance and body member. The system recognizes eight basic motions.

1. Reach (TE)
2. Move (TL)
3. Grasp
4. Turn
5. Position
6. Release Load
7. Apply pressure
8. Disengage

The time taken for the basic motion varies depending on the condition under which it is performed. Time measuring unit = 10 hours = 1/100000 hr = .0006 min =.036 sec

Reach

Move the body member from one place to another place varies with three factors.

1. Length of the motion.
2. Nature of the destination.
3. How the body member
   (*a*) A body member at rest-Rest
   (*b*) Body member Rest-Moving
   (*c*) Body member moving-Rest

Reach 5 classes

<table>
<tr><td>Move</td><td>(a)</td><td>(b)</td><td>(c)</td><td>(d)</td><td>(e)</td></tr>
<tr><td>Grasp</td><td>(a)</td><td>(b)</td><td>(c)</td><td>(d)</td><td>(e)</td></tr>
<tr><td>Position</td><td>(a)</td><td>(b)</td><td>(c)</td><td></td><td></td></tr>
<tr><td colspan="2">(a)</td><td colspan="2">(b)</td><td colspan="2">(c)</td></tr>
<tr><td colspan="2">Alignment
(Bringing to the object)</td><td colspan="2">Orientation
(Must rotate about its own axis)</td><td colspan="2">Engagement</td></tr>
<tr><td colspan="2">Symmetrical
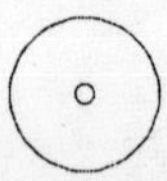</td><td colspan="2">Semi Cylindrical
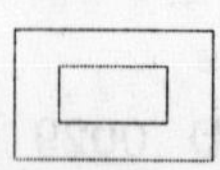</td><td colspan="2">Non Symmetrical</td></tr>
<tr><td colspan="2">Placing</td><td colspan="4">Class of Fit</td></tr>
<tr><td colspan="2"></td><td colspan="4">Size of the object and size of the other part</td></tr>
<tr><td colspan="2">Disengage</td><td colspan="4">Class of Fit, Ease of handling</td></tr>
<tr><td colspan="6">Apply Pressure Simple A.P, A.P with force & re grasp</td></tr>
</table>

8.21 BASIC MOTION TIME STUDY MOTION (BMTS)

Basic motion is defined as a single complete movement of the body member which occurs every time a body member being at rest make a motion or moves over a given distance and again comes to rest. In performing this at any particular time any basic motion the following methods are performed.

1. Distance moved

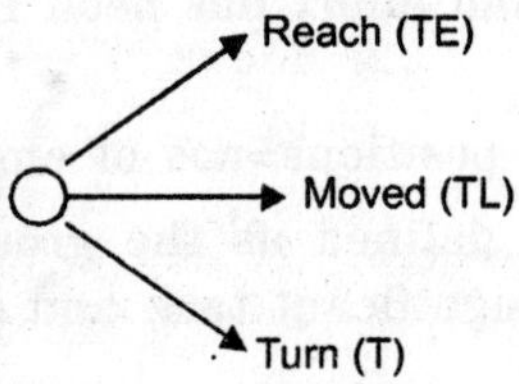

2. In the performance of the basic motion visual attention is required to complete the motion. It may or it may not be there then eye movement is also taken in to consideration.
3. Degree of precision required *i.e.*, care specially if the object is very small in grasping and positioning.
4. For carrying out work some amount of force is needed in handling the object or weight.
5. Simultaneous performance of two basic motion *i.e.*, job difficulty (various factors required to the performance of given motion).

Basic Motion is classified into three classes (By use of body members)

1. **Class A.** The basic motion which is stopped without the use of muscular control or by the impact of another object.
2. **Class B.** Is that basic motion which is entirely stopped by the use of muscular effort (copy can be stopped by lifting or downward stroke of the hammer).
3. **Class C.** Is that motion start by the use of muscular control first for slow down the motion and then end it either in the grasping situation or in a position situation (making example a catch of the boll).

8.22 JOB EVALUATION & MERIT RATING

Relative value basically a Ranking activity finding out the job difficulty involved on the basis of difficulty. In pricing of the job the people carrying out the job. Technical, social, Emotional, security aspects and all short of consideration in the performance of given job. The total activity involves:-

1. Job analysis (What the job consists of).
2. Finding out the relative worth or value of the job for the sake of categorization.
3. Pricing of the job for the sake of establishing salary systems.

Definition. Job Evaluation is defined as the complete operation of determining the value of an individual job in an organization in relation to the other jobs in the organization. It begins with three basic factors. Job analysis is to obtain job description and goals of the job. It also involves the pricing of these values by establishing minimum, maximum salary by each group of job based on there relative value the operation ends with the final checking of the result in salary system. Setting of wages or wage structural and usage incentive plans if we know the structure of the organization. Selection and training of the new employees (what are the requirement of the job) transfer and promotions. It should serve as guidelines to improve employee management relation to develop job satisfaction among the workers.

We define task (whenever some human effort has been involved the effort may be physical/mental).

Definition of Position. Number of positions=nos of employees

Definition of Job. The job can be defined as the group of positions which are identical with respect to there nature or significant task and can be compared for their major contributions.

8.23 JOB EVALUATION METHODS

Non-Quantitative

1. Ranking System
2. Grade Description system

Quantitative Methods

1. Point System
2. Factors comparison systems

Find out the difficulty and job specification and on the basis of that we use the judgement to find out the relative work.

1. Find out the job difficulty.
2. Relative work.
3. Pricing of the job.

Ranking System

1. Selecting the no of jobs to be included in any given job evaluation plan.
2. Job analysis and Job description.
3. Choosing the first Rankers.
4. Ranking the job by the first Ranker.
5. Statistical Treatment of Ranking by first Ranker.
6. Integrating the first ranker. Ranking to develop total/organization ranking.

Jobs are not broken down into their components but are considered as a whole. Jobs are ranked from lowest to highest in terms of their differences in level of duties, responsibilities and requirement and the jobs are compared against each other and then a committee is appointed and asked to rank each job.

Ranking of the Job. By experienced people, people involved in day today activity or finally committee who knows the job.

Statistical Treatment (Paired Comparison Method)

Each job description compared against all jobs in terms of job difficulty say six jobs A B C D E F

Six Jobs A B C D E F

A	A	B		
B	A	C	B	C
C	A	D	B	D
D	A	E	B	E
E	A	F	B	F
F				

Comparison of all jobs *i.e.*, A is compared with B

$$\text{No of Comparison} = \frac{N(N-1)}{2} = \frac{6(6-1)}{2} = \frac{6\times 5}{2} = 15$$

Grade Description Method. Method consists of some short of a standard description of our requirement.

Available Description:

1. Selection of job.
2. Job analysis.
3. Determining the no of levels of standard description.
4. Writing down the standard s grade level description.
5. Assigning the jobs to the grade levels.

Point System Methods

First decided how many category is needed basically consists of the construction of the rating scales which are used for measuring the characteristics.

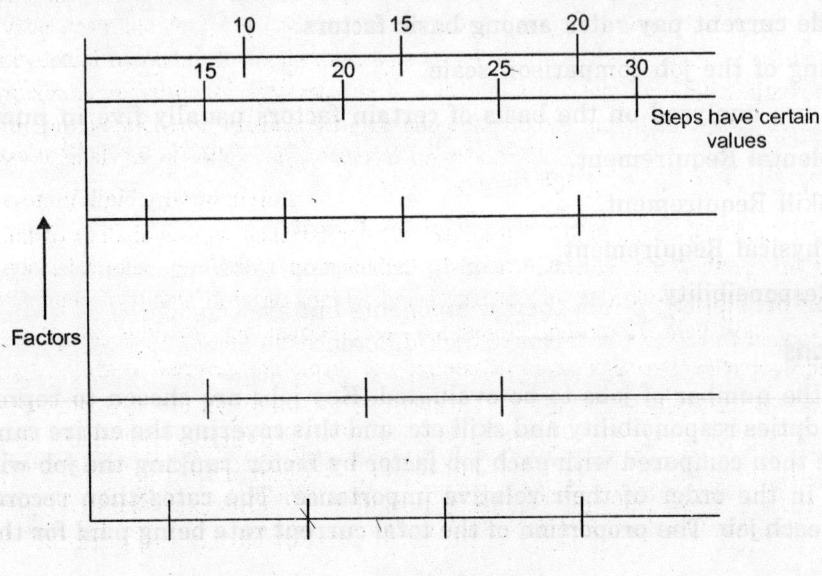

Factors

1. Skill
2. Effort
3. Re-positioning
4. Working condition

The scale to be made depends on the numbers of factors

Steps Involved Area

1. Selection of jobs.
2. Job analysis and job description.
3. Factors and sub factors to be included which are connected to the job.
4. Each factor must be designed at the starting and at the various levels.
5. Determining the steps in each of a factors and their relative value (Defining the degree of each of the factors).
6. Relative value of the factors involved.
7. Assigning the pt values to be degree.

After that find out the relative weight age.

8.24 FACTOR COMPARISION METHOD

1. Numbers of jobs to be included.
2. Job description and Job analysis.
3. Selecting basic factors to be included.
4. Selecting key jobs.
5. Ranking of the key jobs.
6. Divide current pay rates among basic factors.
7. Setting of the job comparison scale.

1. Jobs are analyzed on the basis of certain factors usually five in numbers:
   (*a*) Mental Requirement.
   (*b*) Skill Requirement.
   (*c*) Physical Requirement.
   (*d*) Responsibility.

e-Job Conditions

2-Select the number of jobs to be evaluated. Key jobs are chosen to represent each major level of duties responsibility and skill etc. and this covering the entire range of jobs. These jobs are then compared with each job factor by factor, ranking the job with respect to each other in the order of their relative importance. The rates then recorded under each factor of each job. The proportion of the total current rate being paid for the job. The values assigned. After all the jobs are rated the values assigned for each factor of the job are added together to determine its total value. A wage rate for each job is determined.

Grading of the Marks:

0-25 Marks---Grade I

26-50 Marks---Grade II

51-75 Marks---Grade III

8.25 METHODS OF MERIT RATING

1. Graphic Rating Scale Method.
2. Rankins and Paired Comparison.
3. Man to Man Rating Scale.
4. Free Written Description.
5. Grouping Techniques (Forced Distribution Method)
6. Check List Method

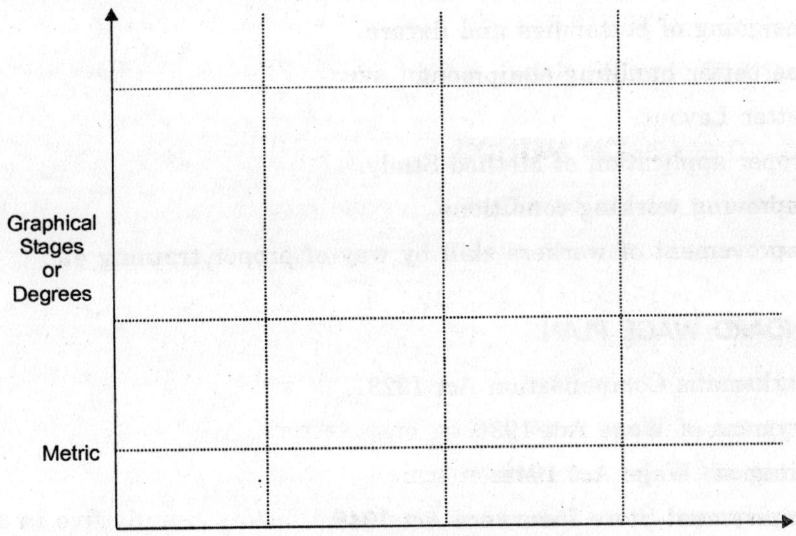

Rankin's and Paired Comparison Method (To compare the people *i.e.*, each person against next and find the best) Only possible for a smallest company.

Man to Man Rating Scale. (4-5 categeaories of a given trade or overall performance are classified and then like a key job have a person is selected for the particular trade) Basically done for a large company (like steel Industries).

Free Written Description. Commonly used in Informal rating peoples are asked to submit bio-data etc. Self evaluation method. Specified characteristics on overall performance.

Grouping Techniques. Like the man to man rating scale categories defines in terms of written statement achieved may be above normal performance etc.

Check List Method. On the basis of various trade features and check list we have to prepare some short of list and compare the performance of man. Example Election rating system. Check the level of achievement from the list. Wage structure on the basis of standard time (Work Measurement).

Wage Incentive. Financial incentive/non financial incentive. Incentive payment on part of the total wages which is paid to the worker in addition to the actual payment. Extra effort put by the workers to this case the level of producing or output.

Minimum Wages. Producing in a less period but producing more.

1. Time Saved /Spent.
2. Effort Put
3. Idea Given

Improvement in use of mechanical equipment, maximum material utilization. Improvement in efficiency/quality. Reducing the Cost etc.

1. Effective utilization of the resources.
2. Effective utilization of the physical facilities.
3. Simplification of system and procedure.
4. Designing of better jigs and fixture.
5. Use better handling equipment.
6. Better Layout.
7. Proper application of Method Study.
8. Improving working conditions.
9. Improvement of workers skill by way of proper training etc.

8.26 STANDARD WAGE PLAN

1. Worksmans Compensation Act 1923.
2. Payment of Wage Act 1936.
3. Minimum Wage Act 1948.
4. Employment State Insurance Act 1948.
5. Real Wages and Money Wages.

Relationship between Wages, Productivity & Cost

Wages—Workers are interested.

Productivity–Management is interested.

Let X = Ratio of producing at any point to 100 Normal or standard production.

X = 1 for 100% Performance Rating

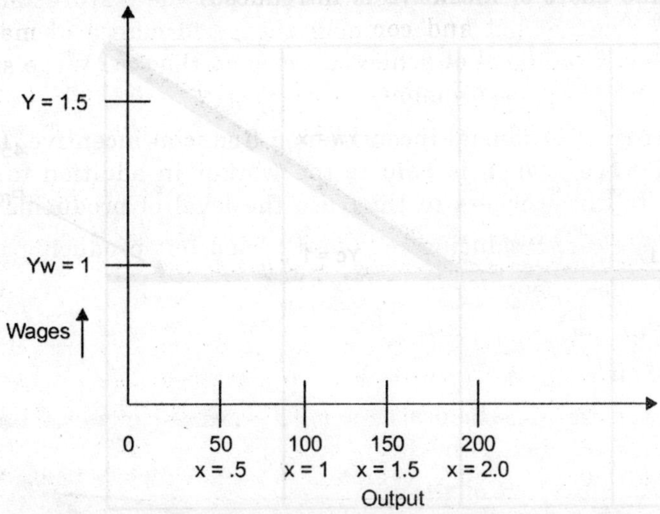

Let Yw = Ratio of wages at any point to the normal or standard wages.

Yc = Ratio of the Labor cost/Mfg cost at any point to the normal or standard cost.

100 part = Rs 100

= 100/100=1 Rs is the standard cost

Yc = Yw/x = 100/100 = Payment/Output = 1

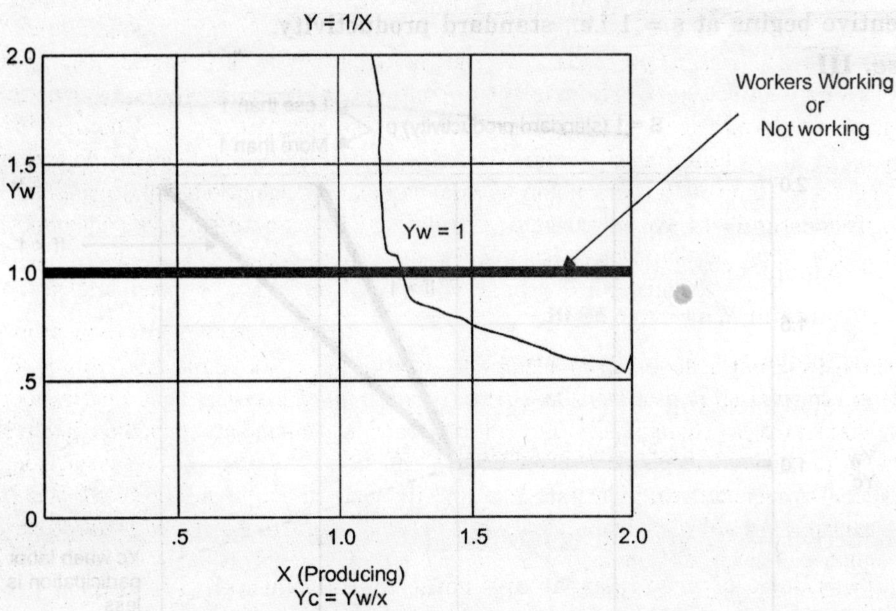

Case. I Days Work (Everybody is paid at the fixed rate)

Then Yc = Yw/x = 1/x, Yw = 1/.5 = 2

Yc = 1/1 = 1 X = 6 Yc = 1/6 = 1.668

Case. II (Some short of incentive is introduced)

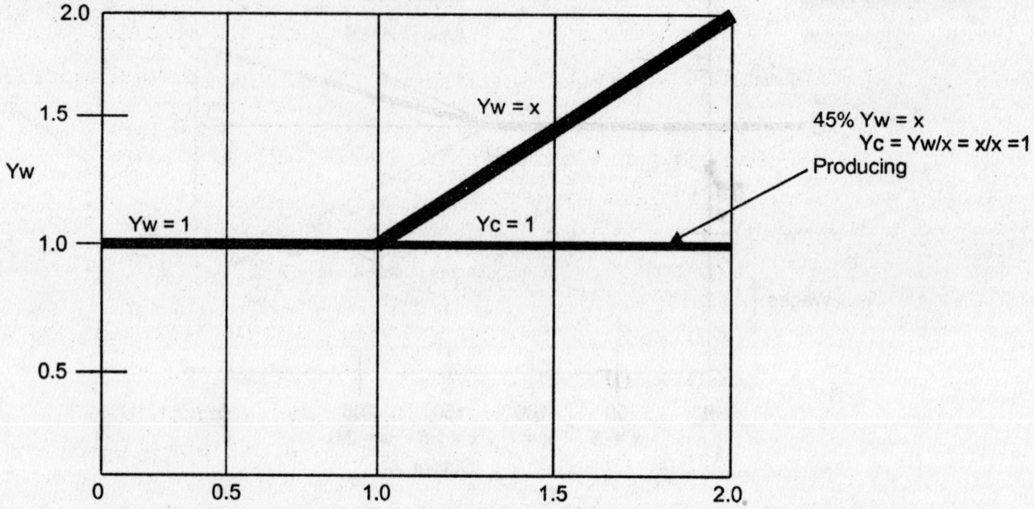

x = 1%- Increase productivity (Incentive paid in such a way that if the worker increases the production by 1% the wages will also increase by 10%

Wages = Yw=1%

X = 1,Yw = 1, Yc = 1

Labòr participation p = 1 (labor participation is also 1)

Incentive begins at s = 1 *i.e.*, standard productivity.

Case. III

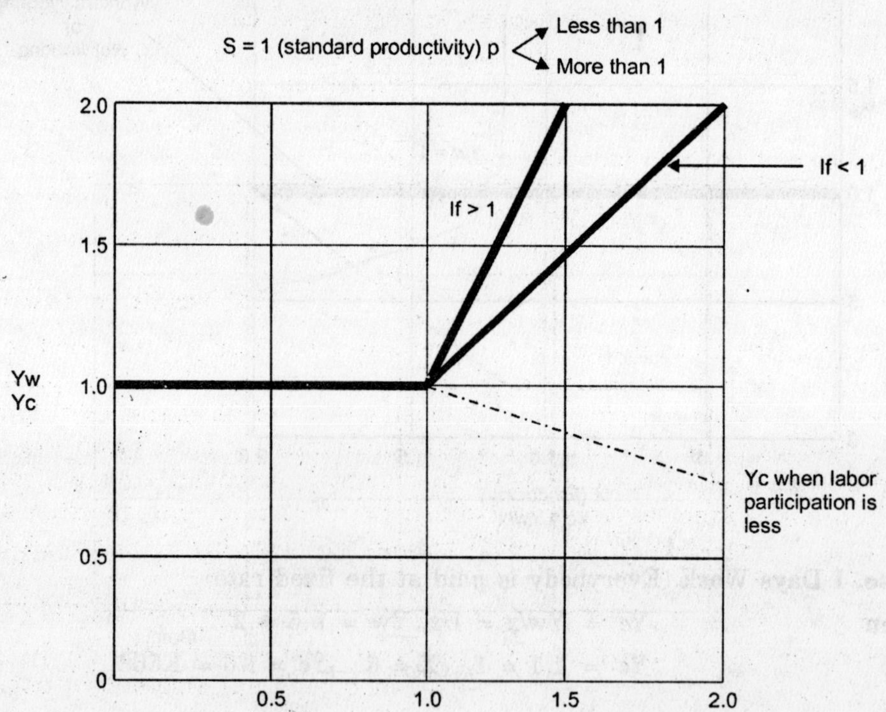

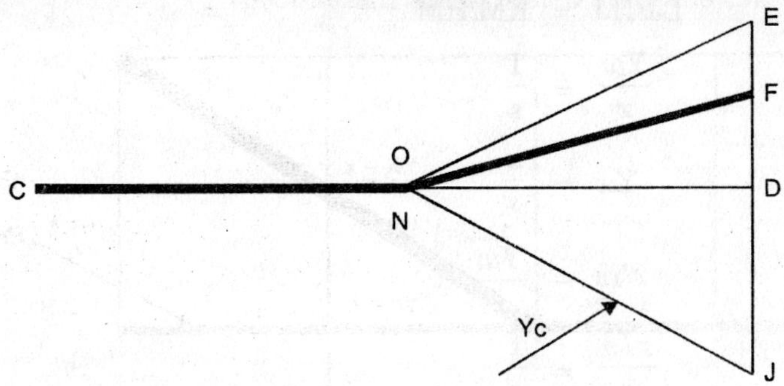

$$CD = X$$

$$OD = DE=ND$$

$$Yw = Fj$$

$$Fj = Dj + FD$$

$$= 1+FD$$

$$FD/DE = p$$

$$FD = p.\ DE$$

$$= p.\ ND$$

$$= p\ (CD-N)$$

$$= p\ (x - 1)\ Yc = \frac{Yw}{x}$$

$$\frac{1+p(X-1)}{x}$$

Case. IV

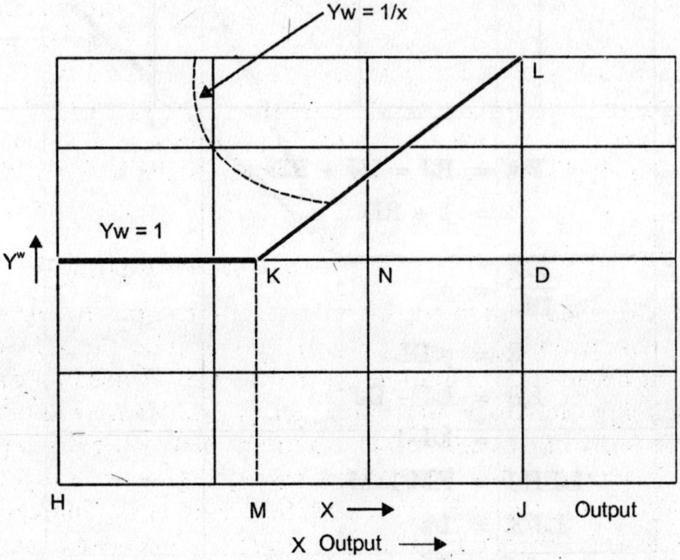

$$LJ/HJ = KM/HM$$

$$\frac{Yw}{x} = \frac{1}{s}$$

$$Yw = \frac{x}{s}$$

$$Yc = \frac{Yw}{x}$$

$$\frac{x/s}{x} = \frac{1}{s}$$

Case. V

Both are not equal to 1

P<1 or more than 1

S<1 or more than1

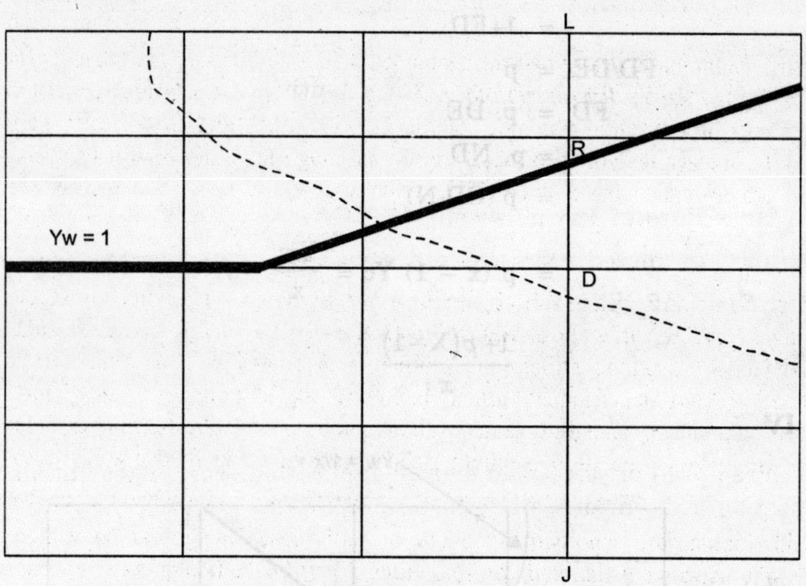

$$Yw = RJ = DJ + RD$$
$$= 1 + RD$$

$$\frac{RD}{DL} = p$$

$$R = p.DL$$

$$LD = LJ - DJ$$
$$= LJ-1$$

$$LJ/HJ = KM/1+M$$

$$LJ/X = 1/s$$

$$LJ = X/s$$

$$LD = LJ\text{-}1$$

i.e., $(x/s - 1)$

$$RJ = DJ + RD$$

$$Yw = 1 + RD$$

$$Yw = 1 + p\ (x/s-1)$$

$$Yc = \frac{1+p(x/s-1)}{x}$$

E = Total earnings in Rs for any establishment period of time one day, month, week etc.

R = Rate of Payment (hrly or day)

H = Actual hrs work

s = Standard time in hrs/piece.

N = No of unit produced in a specified period.

S = Total standard time allowed to produce N part.

P = Piece rate

F = Factor of labor participation with incentive.

First Case–A1

$$E = H.R$$

Actual Hr × Rate of Payment (8hrs × R)

Minimum Guaranteed wages except in case-II *i.e.,* on contract labor only.

Second Case A2 When the company is gaining

$$E = H.R + \%\ HR\ (i.e.,\ \text{some}\ \%\ \text{of}\ HR)$$

$$E = H.R\ (1 + F)$$

Third Case-A3

Job skill required physical and mental application, working condition, local condition, market condition and various other factors.

8.27 STRAIGHT PIECE WORK (100% PRE-PLAN)

$$E = N.P$$

N = Number of Parts

P = Piece Rate

$$= N.\ s.\ R$$

s = Standard time allowed

R = Rate of Payment.

8.28 MERRICK MULTIPLE PIECE PLAN

(Modified to the Taylers Piece rate system). Extra output is to be shared between two parts management and workers.

1. Halsey premium plan

E = H.R (Total accuracy is calculated in terms of the standard time saved)

H-Actual Time

S = Standard time for numbers of parts produced

Time Saved = (S-H)

E = HR + F(S–H) R

H = 25% to 75% varies from situation to situation.

2. Manchester or standard hour plan

E = Daily wages + Incentives

= H.R + some % of HR

HR is calculated in terms of numbers of extra parts produced (S-H)

3. Bedeax point plan

E = HR + .75 (S-H) R

i.e., 1/3 of (S-H) R is paid to the worker directly and .25 (S-H) R kept for welfare methods paid in indirect manner.

PLAN

E = H.R + .5 (S- H) R + .10 (S-H) R+ .40 (S-H) R

(Workers) (Supervisor)

Emerson's and Similar Gain Sharing Plans

The bonus is being at 66 2/3%.If he is producing more than 66 2/3 % then the Bonus is to be paid.

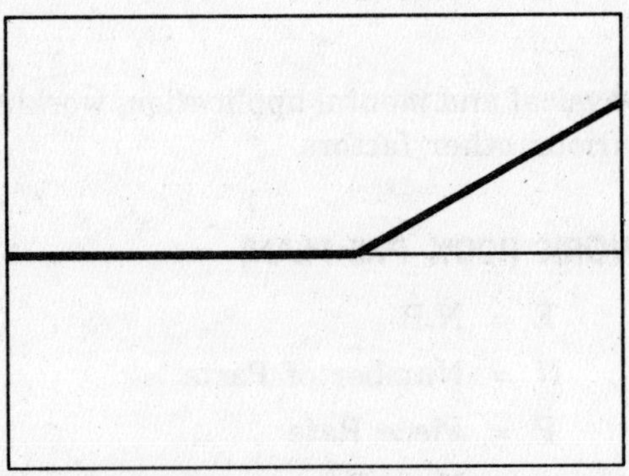

Indirect Worker

By means of calculated Normal Ratio

Ratio between the time allowed by the direct work/Indirect Time taken

= Direct worker time allowed/Indirect Workers

= 1000hrs/500 hrs = 2 hrs

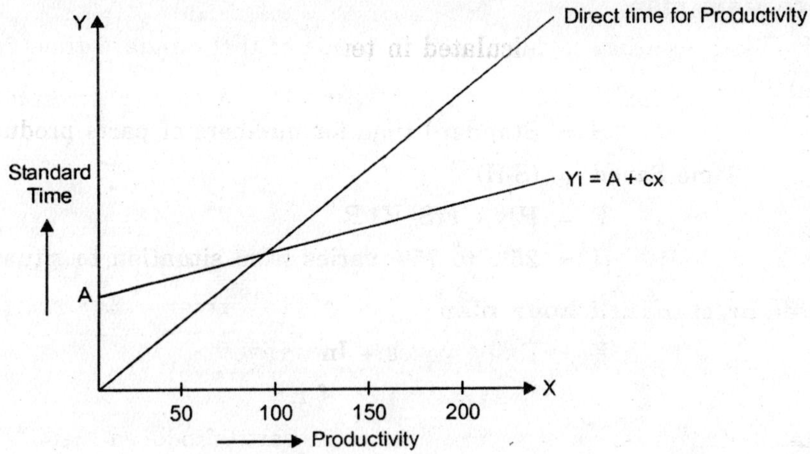

$$Yd = k.\ x$$

$$K = \text{Coefficient}$$

$$X = \text{Productivity}$$

$$R = Yd/Yi = k.\ x/A + c\ x$$

$$10{,}000 \text{ hrs}/5000 = \text{Direct work/Indirect work} = 2.0$$